Defeat

Fear

Forever

Christina Li

Discover other titles by Christina Li at
Amazon.com (print version) and
Smashwords.com (e-book).

Note: For reference **KJV**=The King James
Version of the Bible, **AMP**=The Amplified
Version, **MSG**=The Message Bible, **NIV**=New
International Version, and **NLT**=New Living
Translation

Contents

This book is dedicated to
Amy, Relli, Frankie, Zach, and Kiki.
You are some of the most incredible people I
know!
To my husband Charles.
I love you.
And to my Lord, Savior, and dear Friend.
Jesus, you never stop amazing me.

Introduction

"There is no fear in love; but perfect love casteth out fear: because fear hath torment. He that feareth is not made perfect in love," I John 4:18 (KJV).

So many precious people suffer from fear every day of their lives. I, too, suffered for years without really even knowing it. I thought I was fine. I had the American dream, wonderful husband, great kids, etc. Yet, there were stupid, little things that kept holding me back from what I wanted to accomplish in my life.

I am one of the piano players at our church. We have a wonderful church that I am so blessed to be a part of. However, I wanted to improve my skills. My husband is a professional musician, a violinist. He doesn't play the piano, but he is an amazing coach. With me, unfortunately, I did not take his criticism well. He believed in me, but I didn't believe in myself. Every time he tried to help me, I either argued with him or clammed up. I immediately felt like a failure. That wasn't what my husband wanted for me and it's not what God wanted for me either.

One day, it hit us both, two things really. One was that I was really a negative person. I didn't believe I could actually do it. I didn't believe I could change. The second thing was, because of my personal belief, I didn't really want to even try to change. I didn't have the 'want to'. I realized that I had actually allowed myself to be bound by fear and my subsequent actions (and reactions) were based on that basic belief. Well, God's Word has a little something to say about that.

Philippians 4:13 says, "I can do ALL things through Christ which strengtheneth me," (KJV). Below, I want to show a fun exercise that I read a while ago. Read the whole thing, especially the words in all caps.

I can do all things through Christ which strengtheneth me.
I CAN do all things through Christ which strengtheneth me.
I can DO all things through Christ which strengtheneth me.
I can do ALL things through Christ which strengtheneth me.
I can do all THINGS through Christ which strengtheneth me.
I can do all things THROUGH Christ which strengtheneth me.
I can do all things through CHRIST which strengtheneth me.
I can do all things through Christ which STRENGTHENETH me.

I can do all things through Christ which strengtheneth <u>ME</u>.

I think one of Satan's biggest tools against us is to get us to believe that we can't do something and we simply don't have a choice in the matter. That's just 'the way things are'. Well, I decided to believe all of God's Word and take it for myself. I started believing I really could change, I really could improve. I could be a positive person and I could even get better on the piano. Know what? My playing changed overnight! My husband commented on my touch on the keyboard and how I was better able to communicate with my music. It was amazing. I could hear it too. Playing was actually easier. The interesting thing is, when I started believing in what God could do in my life, my whole life changed. Not only was the piano affected, but my whole world changed.

So, I started being a positive person and I believed I could change. Fear couldn't hold onto me anymore. What a difference. However, that was only the beginning.

Unfortunately, like it or not, there are more things in heaven and earth than we can even imagine. We are in a battle, not of our choosing. Satan and his horde want to take us down. They want to cripple us and keep us from being and doing all that God wants for our lives. Just because I had the victory for a few days didn't mean the battle was over or that I even could keep the victory.

Now, that's not cause for worry. It simply means that getting the victory over fear isn't a one time thing. It's a new mindset. It's creating new habits and gaining a new understanding. This battle was hard won. I want to continue to occupy so Satan cannot retake this ground. I got my victory. I plan on keeping it!

You, too, can have victory over fear— permanently. That's what this little book is all about. God wants this for you.

"Do not pray for easy lives. Pray to be stronger men and women. Do not pray for tasks equal to your powers. Pray for powers equal to your tasks. Then the doing of your work shall be no miracle, but YOU shall be the miracle." --Phillips Brooks

It's time for you to become a miracle. Read on!

Chapter 1
Some Fear is Good?!

"The fear of the Lord is the beginning of wisdom: a good understanding have all they that do his commandments: his praise endureth forever," Psalms 111:10 (KJV).

I don't know about you, but becoming wise seems like a pretty good thing to me. According to the verse above, the fear of the Lord is only the beginning of wisdom. Wisdom, true wisdom, goes much, much deeper. I want to be wise, really wise. I want to have understanding. I want to do His commandments, but not only out of duty, but also out of love and understanding. Why does the Lord's praise endure forever? It is because He gives us wisdom and understanding. He points us in the right direction. He created us. He knows just how much we are capable of. He wants the best for us.

"In the fear of the Lord is strong confidence: and his children shall have a place of refuge," Proverbs 14: 26 (KJV). I struggled for years feeling like I was never good enough. Yet, in the fear of the Lord is strong confidence. When I finally understood this concept, my confidence soared upwards. I didn't have to be afraid anymore. I didn't have to be shy. I could look people in the eye and talk like an intelligent human being, instead of the shy, not-sure-of-herself mouse. I don't know about you, but I think it's a good thing to look in the mirror in the morning and like what I see. It's not about arrogance. It's about confidence—in the Lord and what He is accomplishing in me.

"Being confident of this very thing that he which hath begun a good work in you, will perform it until the day of Jesus Christ," Philippians 1:6 (KJV). God has begun a good work in me. He's not one of those who start something and then forgets about it and leaves it languishing on some shelf. My God finishes what He starts. The great thing is I get to be a part of that work. You see, God doesn't do it all for us. He allows challenges to come our way so that we can grow. Look at difficulties in life as challenges to conquer, opportunities to mature. In every situation, throughout your day, you have a choice in how you will react.

I home-school my five children. Each child has favorite subjects and not-so-favorite subjects. (I've tried very hard to keep them from actually hating any particular subject, but you get the idea.) Anyway, when my youngest is working on her reading and she sounds out the same word for about the fifth time, I can react in several ways. I can get really impatient with her and start raising my voice, 'Why can't you just remember that word?!' Or I can look at this as an opportunity God can use to teach me a lesson too, a lesson in kindness and patience. (Yes, this really did happen.) I decided to not just get louder at the poor kid out of frustration. Instead, I calmly pointed out that it would be a lot easier and faster for her if she just remembered that word. This way she doesn't have to work so hard. She liked that and the next time read through it beautifully. I guess the lesson here is that homeschooling is just as much of an education for me as for the children. I just have to work to be a good student and listen to my Teacher!

"So don't lose a minute in building on what you've been given, complementing your basic faith with good character, spiritual understanding, alert discipline, passionate patience, reverent wonder, warm friendliness, and generous love, each dimension fitting into and developing the others. With these qualities active and growing in your lives, no grass will grow under your feet, no day will pass without its reward as you mature in your experience of our Master Jesus. Without these qualities you can't see what's right before you, oblivious that your old sinful life has been wiped off the books. So, friends, confirm God's invitation to you, his choice of you. Don't put it off; do it now. Do this, and you'll have your life on a firm footing, the streets paved and the way wide open into the eternal kingdom of our Master and Savior, Jesus Christ," II Peter 1:5-11 (MSG). The KJV version of verse 10 puts it this way, "…for if ye do these things, ye shall never fall."

You see, God doesn't call us to fear him and then do nothing. He wants us to work. It's good for us to work. It feels good to work and have a real sense of accomplishment. That's when we start to see ourselves becoming that miracle. The thing is, God will not change us and make us perfect without us choosing that. I have to actually choose to have good character, spiritual understanding, etc. and then act on those choices. If I want to get an 'A' in math, I have to decide to do the studying and work on the problems, then actually DO it!

Some people have this crazy idea that God will help them pass their courses in school (or whatever in life) without studying. They don't read the textbook or show up for class and think a quick prayer on the day of the test is going to do it for them.

Sorry, it doesn't work like that. God won't cheat! He helps us; He doesn't do our work for us. In order to get good character, I have to choose to be good. I have to make good choices. In order to get spiritual understanding, I have to study God's Word. In order to have alert discipline, I have to choose to be alert. I have to choose to discipline myself. In order to have passionate patience, I have to choose to be patient rather than shouting out my frustration. I can actually smile through the little frustrations of the day and it feels good to get that victory! I have to choose to have reverent wonder and warm friendliness and generous love. It feels good to choose to be good. Believe me, my husband and children are much happier too (and easier to get along with!). The whole atmosphere of our home is changed.

You've heard the saying, 'If Momma ain't happy, ain't nobody happy.' That's true. My attitude is very contagious. If I want to pass on victory to my children, I have to demonstrate getting the victory now. If I want my husband to want to come home, I need to make my home a place that's nice to come home to.

This morning my husband and I were discussing how to help our children deal with their frustration. Growing up, I tended to be somewhat argumentative (My husband would say that's putting it mildly!). One of my teachers in school thought I should become a lawyer. The problem is that tendency has become a habit with me. More unfortunately, it's a habit I'm passing on to our children. During this morning's discussion, I began to feel condemned. You see, my husband was saying that I was perpetuating the children's behavior because I was tending to argue with them. Not only was I contributing, but I had modeled this for them. The problem was he was absolutely right and I hated to admit it!

Being the wonderful, perceptive man that he is, finally he asked me what was wrong. I told him I felt bad because of what he was saying. He asked me if I felt convicted or condemned. This question was crucial. I realized that I was feeling condemned. Well, God doesn't ever condemn us. He convicts us so that we can change our ways and become better. If I'm feeling condemned, that can only be from one source—Satan. I have power over Satan. I can cast him out in Jesus' name, which I promptly did. Wow! Instantly, I had the victory. My peace was back and all fear and other nasty feelings were gone. This enabled me to look at my husband's words and realize that yes, he was right, but that I could change. I had the power to change.

Now, that doesn't mean that our children's behavior will change overnight. It's going to take a few days. There are also my own bad habits to deal with as well. I need to recognize when I'm falling into my own bad habit of arguing and stop instantly, modeling good habits rather than bad ones. You see, I can't just tell my children they are arguing or that they have a bad attitude. I need to model for them proper ways of discussing issues and maintaining a good attitude, but I can't stop there. I also have to teach them how to do this for themselves.

Bottom line? In order to defeat fear forever, the first step is to fear the Lord and work to become like Him. Joy Haney in her book, *At the Master's Feet*, says, "To fear the Lord is to respect His Word and to obey it. It is to walk softly before God with great reverence and awe at His glory and presence. It is to set Him up on the highest throne of your heart—to exalt Him and worship Him continually." If I consistently do this, I will never fear.

"The Lord is my light and my salvation; whom shall I fear: the Lord is the strength of my life; of whom shall I be afraid? When the wicked, even mine enemies and my foes, came upon me to eat up my flesh, they stumbled and fell. Though an host should encamp against me, my heart shall not fear: though war should rise against me, in this will I be confident. One thing have I desired of the Lord, that will I seek after; that I may dwell in the house of the Lord all the days of my life, to behold the beauty of the Lord, and to enquire in his temple. For in the time of trouble he shall hide me in his pavilion: in the secret of his tabernacle shall he hide me; he shall set me up upon a rock. And now shall mine head be lifted up above mine enemies round about me: therefore will I offer in his tabernacle sacrifices of joy; I will sing, yea, I will sing praises unto the Lord," Psalm 27:1-6 (KJV).

Psalm 27 is one of my favorite Psalms. To pay for college, I joined the Air National Guard. At the time, no one had any idea that war was looming on the horizon. I figured one weekend a month and two weeks a year for six years was not much to ask for having my entire college bachelor's degree covered. Then, the Gulf War happened. I admit it, I was scared. The verses in Psalm 27 were a great comfort to me at that time. I knew that no matter what happened, God was still in control and He would never leave me. As it turned out, the war ended days before my unit was to be shipped out.

"The fear of the Lord tendeth to life: and he that hath it shall abide satisfied; he shall not be visited with evil," Proverbs 19:23 (KJV). Now, I don't like evil anymore than anybody else. I certainly don't want to be visited by it! Well, the Lord promises protection and not just drab, scary, run-and-hide protection, but He promises LIFE and abiding satisfied. That means living and having all our needs met. After a good meal, sitting back from the table and rubbing your stomach, satisfied, that's what life with Jesus is. In effect, fearing the Lord makes us untouchable, even invincible.

Proverbs 3:26 says, "For the Lord shall be thy confidence, and shall keep thy foot from being taken," (KJV). When I fear God, I don't have to be afraid of anything. I love this next story I read in Joy Haney's book, *At the Master's Feet*. "During an earthquake a few years ago, the inhabitants of a small village were very much alarmed. One old woman, whom they all knew, was surprisingly calm and joyous. At length, one of them said to her, 'Mother, are you not afraid?' 'No,' she answered. 'I rejoice to know that I have a God who can shake the world.'"

There's one last thing I want to bring to your attention before we end this chapter. That is this important fact: there is a difference between 'fear of the Lord' and 'bondage to fear'. In the Introduction I quoted I John 4:18, "There is no fear in love; but perfect love casteth out fear: because fear hath torment. He that feareth is not made perfect in love," (KJV). You see, God loves us. He isn't about torment. He wants what is best for us. His love will never put us in bondage. In fact, God wants to liberate us.

Fearing God changes our perspective. It causes us to think beyond the scope of ourselves and look to Someone greater. You see, the dreams I have for myself are so much smaller than the dreams God has for me. I actually limit myself by holding onto my own ideas and refusing to consider the Lord in my life. If I take my focus off myself and my own ideas and put it on Him, it's then that I start to become truly free—from fear and whatever else is holding me back. I am finally able to soar. Essentially, I acknowledge that I really can't control my life. I need help. It's when I let Jesus take over the pilot seat that miracles happen.

Do you want hope in your life? Real hope? The only place it can be found is in Jesus Christ. This world has a lot of nice things to offer, but in the end, it all turns to dust. Jesus said, "I am the way, and the truth, and the life," John 14:6 (KJV). I want direction in my life. I want to be able to distinguish truth from lies. I want LIFE to my life. I don't want to just survive, I want to thrive. This can only be found in Jesus.

I've tried other things. I've even looked at some of the other religions out there. I won't slam them, but I will say that my God is real and that He wants to know me…and you. You see, it's not really about religion, it's about relationship. When we stand before God at the end of our lives, will He say, "Welcome!" Or will He say, "Depart from me, I never KNEW you!"

The most important thing right now is to get to know God. His name is Jesus and that means, 'God has become my savior'. It all comes back to the fact that God LOVES you and me. It's all about having a relationship with Someone who already knows all your faults (so it's useless to try to hide them from Him), but He loves you anyway. In fact, the truth is God loves you just the way you are, but He loves you too much to let you stay that way! Do you really want to stay the way you are right now? I mean, I'm pretty excited about what God has done in my life so far, but I hope to be a whole lot more wise, noble, and kind in the years to come.

I want to be more like Jesus. When He walked the earth as a human being, He never sinned. He was perfect, yet never arrogant, never unkind. He was…simply wonderful to have around and to be around. I want to be like that, and to truly be a blessing to all the special people the Lord has put into my life.

A relationship with God is never stagnant. It's vibrant and growing, all about change, and challenge. It's about getting to be that miracle to yourself. You can defeat fear forever. It all comes down to really getting to know the One who can help you.

This chapter has been about good fear—the fear of the Lord. As you get to know Him, you will learn to become truly victorious in your life. In the next chapter, I'm going to discuss bad fear, what it is, where it comes from, and what it causes us to do.

Chapter 2
Bad Fear

Romans 8:15 says, "For ye have not received the spirit of bondage again to fear; but ye have received the Spirit of adoption, whereby we cry, Abba, Father."

When you compare the word 'fear' found in Romans 8:15 with the word fear found in Proverbs 14:26, "In the fear of the Lord is strong confidence: and his children shall have a place of refuge," (KJV), you will see that they are actually two very different words. The fear in Proverbs means 'reverence', while the word fear in Romans means 'terror'. In the last chapter, we talked about the fact that God is not about terror. God is about love. Now, he is big and powerful, but He's not out to get us.

Unfortunately, Fear, the 'terror' kind, can lead to some very bad decisions. For instance, the story of Lot and his family is not a pretty one. (This story can be found in Genesis 19.) Lot went with his Uncle Abraham to the land God had promised. As both men grew more and more prosperous, their servants started fighting with each other over water rights. So, Abraham and Lot had a talk and one went one direction and the other went the other direction, thus dividing the land in half. Abraham was very gracious and let Lot choose. Lot wasn't so gracious and chose what he thought was the better half. Unfortunately, this got him into a lot of trouble.

Lot and his family moved into a very corrupt city. Eventually, God decided to destroy the city completely. Abraham petitioned on Lot's behalf and God sent angels to rescue him and his family. Good news, Lot, his wife, and his daughters got out of the city limits. Bad news, Lot's wife didn't really want to leave, so she disobeyed the angels and was turned into a pillar of salt. (It wasn't a pretty statue looking thing either!) More bad news, Lot's daughters' husbands did not get out. It gets worse.

Lot was so scared at the destruction of the city and the death (judgment) on his wife that he took his daughters up into some mountains to live in caves. Guess what? It gets even worse! The daughters weren't getting any younger and wanted to have children. (Back then, it was really bad for women to not have children.) Anyway, because of Lot's fear, his daughters were denied the opportunity to get remarried. He could've talked to Abraham, but he didn't. Lot had options; he just didn't go to God and ask for help. So, his daughters took matters into their own hands, got their father drunk and had sexual relations with him. Fear was the seed. His daughters' actions were the consequences.

Fear often paralyzes us and causes us to do horrible things. Even Abraham did some pretty stupid things because of his fears. He had to pass through Egypt a couple of times. Sarah, his wife, was very beautiful. Abraham was afraid that the pharaoh would want Sarah and try to get rid of him, permanently. So, he told Sarah to tell the king that she was his sister. Instead of telling the truth and asking God to protect him, Abraham took matters into his own hands. When the pharaoh found out, he was not happy. Basically, he booted both Abraham and Sarah out of the country. It could have been much worse.

Another time Abraham was afraid was when God told him he would have a child in his old age. Now, both Abraham and Sarah were significantly advanced in age. Sarah was in her eighties. Physically, there was no way for her to even get pregnant, much less carry to term. So, after a couple of years, Abraham got scared and talked himself into 'helping' God to fulfill His promise. Sarah was in on it. She told Abraham to take her servant girl as a wife and have a child through her. This was a really bad idea in so many ways. First off, a man doesn't need more than one wife. (I certainly wouldn't share!) Second, Sarah ended up becoming very jealous of her servant girl who did get pregnant and gave Abraham a son.

Because of this 'change in status', the servant girl became very disrespectful of her former mistress. It was a really bad scene. Finally, Sarah talked Abraham into booting the servant girl and her son out of the camp completely. (Abraham and his family were nomadic and lived like Bedouins in large tents.) If God hadn't intervened, she and her child would have died in the desert.

Because of Abraham and Sarah's fear, they acted in some despicable ways. Remember, this kind of fear involves terror, torment, and slavery. This is of Satan and he hates all humans. He actually enjoys it when we suffer. He will take any shot at us he can. Satan and Fear are 'bosom' buddies.

Fear always lies in wait, ready to pounce on us when we let down our guard. A good example of this happened to the prophet Elijah. He was a prophet of God who loved Him very much and followed Him with all of his heart. In I Kings 18 Elijah challenged the worshippers of Baal to a contest. Each was to set up a sacrifice and the God who was real would send down the fire to burn it up.

The Baal worshippers agreed and got their sacrifice ready. They worshipped and did all kinds of things to get their god to answer them and send down a little spark their way. Nothing happened. The Baal worshippers even started cutting themselves to show their devotion. Elijah couldn't resist a good opportunity, so he added insult to injury and suggested that perhaps Baal was busy—in the bathroom—doing his business. Eventually, the Baal worshippers gave up and let Elijah have his turn.

They probably thought nothing would happen for him either. Elijah, however, decided to take things several steps further. He had some folks bring several barrels of water and pour it over his sacrifice (making it harder to burn). When it was good and sopping wet, Elijah prayed. Well, my God is very real and He responded to Elijah's prayer. Not only was the sacrifice burnt up, but the entire altar, stones and all, went up in flames as well. In fact, the stones melted in the intense heat. Obviously, Elijah won that battle.

However, the queen of the land was not pleased at all. She was a very evil woman and did not like Elijah calling her on her immoral behavior. She issued an edict that made Elijah a dead man.

Now, Elijah had just experienced a great victory. Yet, when he heard of this woman's command, he got scared and ran, and ran, and ran. In fact, he ran for several days. Fear saw an opportunity and leaped on it. Elijah ended up hiding out in a cave having a pity party. He even asked God to just let him die.

Have you ever felt that way? I know I have. The root of this is Fear.

However, God did not leave Elijah and He will not leave you, either. The rest of that story is that God spoke to Elijah and gave him some marching orders of what to do next in his life, (anoint a couple of men as kings and a prophet to follow after him). God showed him that he was not the only one left who still loved the Lord and served Him. (Fear lied to Elijah and made him think he was all alone.) God showed Elijah the truth. There were seven thousand men who still obeyed and served the One True God. Elijah was never alone. There was still a lot of hope.

You see, what happened with Elijah, and what can happen to us as well, is that he took his eyes off the Lord and put them on his fears. Fear lied to him and distracted him. Once Elijah had taken his eyes off the Lord, he was an easy target.

"In the fear of the Lord is strong confidence: and his children shall have a place of refuge," Proverbs 14:26 (KJV).

We can have confidence by fearing or reverencing the Lord, and not just confidence, but strong confidence. God had sent fire down from heaven for Elijah. Think what might have been had Elijah been bold. What difference would that have made for the nation of Israel?

Perhaps they would've gotten rid of the corrupt king and queen much sooner. Who knows? Perhaps Elijah would have been a part of more miracles. During his lifetime, Elijah is credited with fourteen miracles if you include the prophecies. Could there have been more had Elijah not allowed himself to become afraid? We'll never know.

Deuteronomy 31:8 says, "And the Lord, he it is that doth go before thee; he will be with thee, he will not fail thee, neither forsake thee: fear not, neither be dismayed," (KJV).

Young's Literal Translation puts the verse above this way, "and Jehovah [is] He who is going before thee, He himself is with thee; He doth not fail thee nor forsake thee; fear not, nor be affrighted."

What I like about the verse above is the fact that God actually goes before us. He sees what trouble there is long before we do. He is already there and prepared for it. What do we need to be afraid of? Not only does God get there first, He goes in with us. We never have to face any trial alone. God is there. He, Himself, is there with us. Indeed, God will never fail or forsake us.

We are commanded to fear not, neither be dismayed. The Amplified Bible puts Deuteronomy 31: 8 this way, "It is the Lord Who goes before you; He will [march] with you; He will not fail you or let you go or forsake you; [let there be no cowardice or flinching, but] fear not, neither become broken [in spirit—depressed, dismayed, and unnerved with alarm]."

Fear is a choice (or God would not command us to 'fear not'). We can choose whether we are fearful or fearless, flinching or unflinching, cowardly or courageous. We get to choose whether or not we become broken in spirit. We can say no to depression, dismay and alarm. Make no mistake, we always have a choice. Fear will lie and say, "This is the way it is, you have no choice," but that is simply not true.

Matthew 10:28-31 says, "Don't be bluffed into silence by the threats of bullies. There's nothing they can do to your soul, your core being. Save your fear for God, who holds your entire life—body and soul—in his hands.

"What's the price of a pet canary? Some loose change, right? And God cares what happens to it even more than you do. He pays even greater attention to you, down to the last detail—even numbering the hairs on your head! So don't be intimidated by all this bully talk. You're worth more than a million canaries," (MSG).

When you get right down to it, fear is nothing more than a bully. The Bible says Satan prowls

27

around like a roaring lion, seeking whom he may devoir. I Peter 5:8 says, "Be well balanced (temperate, sober of mind), be vigilant and cautious at all times; for that enemy of yours, the devil, roams around like a lion roaring [in fierce hunger], seeking someone to seize upon and devour," (AMP).

The lion that roars is really the old one, with no teeth. He roars to scare his prey into running. The prey runs away from the sound of the roar and right to the younger lions, hiding in wait. With Satan, there are no 'younger lions hiding in wait'. He's looking around for someone who has their guard down, someone weak, that he can pounce upon. The thing is, God is greater and He gives us all the power we need. We don't have to fall prey to Satan and his tricks. Satan is just a big, ugly bully. He can't hurt you. He can only lie to you and try to make you think he can hurt you. He's all bluff. Only Jesus has real power. Satan would like people to think he has real power, but that's just not true. The only people Satan can hurt are those that let him.

Jesus is the only one, true God. Satan tried to hurt Him by getting the people to crucify him, but it didn't work. Jesus didn't stay dead! He rose in victory, not just for Himself, but for you and me.

In this spiritual battle, Satan and his followers are the losers. His time is short and he knows it. He wants to take as many people down with him as will let him. What will you choose?

It IS your choice. Which will you choose to believe, Fear or Faith? Which will you look at, your problems or the Solution? Who will you follow, the spirit of Fear or the Spirit of the one true God, the living, almighty Savior, Jesus?

In this chapter we discussed 'Bad Fear', what it is, what it can cause us to do, and the choice that we have. We discussed what can happen when we focus on our fears rather than on the One who always goes before us and is always with us, the One who will never fail or forsake us. In the next chapter we will discuss the fact that fear is a choice and what we can do about it. Read on!

Chapter 3
Fear is a Choice

"Fear thou not; for I am with thee: be not dismayed; for I am thy God: I will strengthen thee; yea, I will help thee; yea, I will uphold thee with the right hand of my righteousness." Isaiah 41:10.

Remember when I said earlier in this book that one of Satan's biggest weapons is getting us to believe his lies? One of his biggest lies is that we have no choice. Friends, that is simply not true. Yes, there is that 'feeling' of fear that sometimes comes upon us, but we have every choice in how we will act. There are myriads of stories that tell of what heroes did in the face of fear. When we feel fear coming at us with both guns blazing, are we going to cower in a hole somewhere inside of ourselves, or are we going to fight?

In my life, I've been held back so many, many times because of fear. I didn't even try sometimes because of my own fears. There comes a time when we need to say to ourselves this will stop now. It doesn't matter what the world throws my way. It doesn't matter what the devil throws my way, I will choose to not live in fear.

Isaiah was an amazing prophet. Like most prophets, he often had the unhappy task of telling people things that they didn't want to hear. He probably felt afraid numerous times, yet he still obeyed God. In the verse above (Isaiah 41:10), God commands the Jewish people to 'fear not'. It's not a suggestion. It's a command. Though this verse is written to the Jewish people several thousand years ago, it still applies to us today.

God doesn't leave it there with just a simple command, however. He goes on to say why they don't need to be afraid. It is because He is their God. He is our God. He has chosen us to be His people and He takes care of His own just as you and I take care of our own children. How many times in the night have my husband or I been woken up by a frightened child? We were quick to comfort them and let them know that we wouldn't let anything happen to them. God is the same with us. God even goes further and says he will strengthen us. He will uphold us with the right hand of His righteousness. Now, there is some serious power there!

The Amplified Version puts Isaiah 41:10 nicely, "Fear not [there is nothing to fear], for I am with you; do not look around you in terror and be dismayed, for I am your God. I will strengthen you and harden you to difficulties, yes, I will help you; yes I will hold you up and retain you with My [victorious] right hand of rightness and justice."

Keep in mind, God already knows the end from the beginning. He already has the victory. He knows our troubles before we do. He doesn't want us to be continually afraid and worried and fretting. He doesn't want us to be looking around for help. He's right there. He's right HERE. He has chosen us. He wants to help us. He can strengthen us and 'harden' us to difficulties, if we let Him. However, we need to let Him. He will never force Himself upon us. If we choose to live in fear and worry, He won't force us out of that. He offers us a way out, if we choose that. If my child still chooses to be afraid of whatever, there is really nothing I can do to change that. I can comfort her and hold her, but she has to let go of her fear and trust me. She has to believe me when I tell her I won't let anything happen to her.

Some of the trials in this life can seem pretty daunting, even life threatening. There is the threat of disease, war, financial loss and hardship, loss of a loved one. The list goes on and on, yet we have a choice in how we choose to live. Will I live in fear or trust? Will you live in fear or trust?

Daniel is one of my favorite prophets. He was taken into captivity when Israel was overthrown by the Babylonians. I'm sure he felt a lot of fear. These people had the power to end his life at any moment. Yet God preserved his life and even caused him to be favored. His first 'test' came when he and three other young Hebrew men were commanded to eat of the king's meat. However, God had some specific food laws and the king's meat was considered 'unclean'. (Sanitation was different back then. So, God had set up some strict dietary laws for the Jews' preservation.) Anyway, Daniel and his friends asked the guards in charge of them if they could eat only vegetables and other foods that were not unclean. They weren't arrogant or belligerent about asking, but instead were very polite. They asked that they be given a certain amount of time on their diet and if they weren't healthy, they would obey the king's command. The guard, reluctantly, agreed. After the time was up, Daniel and his friends were actually healthier than the others around them. First test, passed!!

Another test came about several years, and a different king, later. Daniel was able to interpret a dream the king had that no one else could. The other advisors to the king were very jealous, so they devised a plan to have Daniel killed. They got the king to sign a proclamation that no one was to worship anything or anyone except him for thirty days. Anyone who disobeyed would be thrown into a den of lions.

It would have been so easy for Daniel to just comply with the ruling and pray to his God in secret, but he did not. He heard the edict, knew the ramifications, and went right on praying to his God just as before. Daniel knew his God. He knew that his God would strengthen him and help him and uphold him with His right hand. So, the jealous advisors caught Daniel in the act of praying not to the king, but to his God. Now, Daniel knew this would happen. The edict was to last for thirty days. It was only a matter of time before he was caught. Because of Babylonian law, there was nothing the king could do about it, either. So, Daniel was tossed into a den of lions.

I'm sure he must've been a little nervous. Have you ever seen a lion up close at the zoo? These are not cuddly, little kitty cats. These are big, ferocious beasts with sharp teeth and claws. They are bigger and stronger than men. They weigh more then men do too. One lion could kill Daniel in seconds. He was thrown into a den with several. Know what their keepers did to ensure the lions would eat whatever was thrown down? They kept them hungry. I don't know about you, but I can get rather grouchy when I'm hungry. So, you have one man thrown into a den with several hungry, angry lions.

But God stepped in. Daniel was never alone, not for one moment. God knew all along what would happen and was ready for it. "And when he (the king) came to the den, he cried with a lamentable voice unto Daniel: and the king spake and said to

Daniel, O Daniel, servant of the living God, is thy God, whom thou servest continually, able to deliver thee from the lions? Then said Daniel unto the king, O king, live forever. My God hath sent his angel, and hath shut the lions' mouths, that they have not hurt me: forasmuch as before him innocency was found in me; and also before thee, O king, have I done no hurt. Then the king was exceeding glad for him, and commanded that they should take Daniel up out of the den. So Daniel was taken up out of the den, and no manner of hurt was found upon him, because he believed in his God." Daniel 6:20-23 (KJV).

Daniel was delivered because he believed in his God. Just as our children trust us completely and utterly, we need to trust our God. Jesus has the power to deliver us. He has all power. What would've happened if Daniel hadn't trusted? Who knows, but we probably wouldn't be reading about him today. What an example for us. In the face of certain death, Daniel trusted completely. He stood firm on what God had commanded and God delivered him.

Another great example of bravery in the face of certain death can be found in the accounts concerning Daniel's three friends, also Hebrews taken into slavery at the same time he was. Their names were Hananiah, Mishael, and Azariah. You might know them as Shadrach, Meshach, and Abednego.

Their story takes place in Daniel Chapter 3. At this time, the king decided to make a huge statue out of gold. At a certain time, at the sound of the trumpets, everyone, and I mean everyone, was to bow down to it and worship. If a person did not bow down and worship, he was to be thrown into a fiery furnace.

The temptation, I'm sure was to just give the statue lip service and 'not really mean it'. However, for these Jewish men, their God was just too precious to do that. They couldn't deny Him like that. Simply put, they would worship Him and no other, no matter what. Of course the king did not take this well. He was angry, very angry. Therefore, he had his men turn up the heat in the furnace seven times hotter. Then, he had Shadrach, Meshach, and Abednego thrown in. The furnace was so hot, some of the men who threw them into the furnace died. However, Shadrach, Meshach, and Abednego were completely unharmed. In fact, their bonds were loosed and it looked as if they were walking around in there—with Someone else. Finally, the king commanded them to be let out. When they were examined, not even a hair on their heads was singed!

This is the power that our God has. It doesn't matter what the world throws at us. It doesn't matter how mean and nasty the boss is, God is greater. It doesn't matter how fiery your trial is, Jesus is God Almighty, and He is GREATER. He will even walk through that fiery trial with you. Just trust him.

Mark 5:36 says, "Be not afraid, only believe." These are the words of Jesus to a leader in the synagogue (Jewish church). His daughter had just died and everyone around him was wailing and crying. This man wanted a miracle from Jesus. He loved his daughter very much and didn't want her to die. Jesus put all the people out except three of His disciples and the mother and father. "…He went in where the little girl was lying. Gripping her [firmly] by the hand, He said to her, Talitha cumi—which translated is, Little girl, I say to you, arise [from the sleep of death]! And instantly the girl got up and started walking around—for she was twelve years old. And they were utterly astonished and overcome with amazement." (Mark 5: 40-42, Amplified).

That leader in the synagogue had two choices. He could continue to be afraid or he could do as Jesus said and "just believe." All the evidence supported being very afraid. His daughter had been pronounced dead. The mourners were at the house already! Believing in the face of all that went against common sense. Yet, that was what Jesus asked him to do. In effect, Jesus told this man to hope against all hope. That is exactly what the man did and he got his miracle.

In the above three stories, we've seen examples of men who were delivered because they trusted their God. I want to show you a story where a man seemingly did not get his miracle, yet he still believed. In the face of death, this man continued trusting the Lord. This is the story of Stephen, told in the book of Acts, chapters 6-8. He was a devout man who loved the Lord Jesus very much. He was witnessing to others about the power of Jesus and the fact that He is God. This did not make the synagogue leaders happy. They brought him in and questioned him. Stephen gave an incredible sermon starting with the prophets and ending with the crucifixion. He accused them of killing the Messiah. Those men were cut to the heart, but instead of repenting of their sins, they decided to stone Stephen. The interesting thing is Stephen was never afraid. In fact, in his final moments, he asked for mercy for the men who were stoning him! Stephen died, still trusting God.

On the surface it looks as if God 'let Stephen down'. He trusted God, but God didn't deliver him. We need to realize that this life is not all there is. Like it or not, we all have an incurable disease. No matter what we do, where we go, how much money or things we have, we will all someday die. However, because of Jesus, we have hope for life after death. We know that we will not suffer anymore. We can enjoy everlasting life with Him. Keep trusting. Keep believing. Ultimately, even in the face of what seems impossible, God has something for you beyond your wildest imagination. That is the hope we can all cling to.

These miracles aren't just fun reading. They still happen today, despite what some may say. We see miracles in our church all the time. The Bible is clear: "And these signs shall follow them that believe..." (Mark 16:17). If we trust God, amazing things will happen. If we only believe, God will strengthen us, help us, and uphold us with the right hand of His righteousness.

There was a little girl who had never walked before. My mother-in-law worked at the hospital as an interpreter and told us about her. She wanted us to come and pray for her. My four year old son and husband went and put their hands on her head and shoulders, just like it says in the Bible, and prayed for her. At the time, they couldn't see any obvious changes. They just had to walk by faith.

About a week later, my husband got a phone call from my mother-in-law. She was weeping so she could hardly speak. At first my husband was afraid someone had been hurt. When she was finally able to speak, she said, "Emily is walking!" It was a miracle. There was no denying it. We all got to see her several days later. What a beautiful little girl! She used a walker, but then, she was learning to walk for the very first time in her life. It was an amazing sight to see. We still get Christmas cards from her and her family. To this day, she is walking just fine.

In this chapter, we discussed the fact that fear is a choice. Every day, every moment of every day, you have a choice to make. Will you believe Fear or will you believe the Truth that can set you free? I know it can be hard. I'm not saying it's not a fight, because it is. However, you have the power to get the victory here, but you have to choose to be victorious.

Hebrews 11:1 says it well: "Now faith is the substance of things hoped for, the evidence of things not seen," (KJV). The Amplified version says it this way: "Now faith is the assurance (the confirmation, the title deed) of the things [we] hope for, being the proof of things [we] do not see and the conviction of their reality [faith perceiving as real fact what is not revealed to the senses]."

Like it or not, faith takes work. It takes a determined mindset. Faith demands action. I can say I have all the faith in the world that a certain chair will hold me, but until I actually sit down, I'm not really exercising my faith. Bottom line: If you really believe something, the actions you take in your life will reflect that belief.

In the next chapter, we will discuss the weapons available to us to get down and not only fight Fear, but Defeat Fear Completely and Forever! Read on!

Chapter 4
Weapons Available to Help
Us Defeat Fear
Utterly and Completely

II Timothy 1:7: "For God hath not given us the spirit of fear; but of power, and of love, and of a sound mind," (KJV). The Amplified Version puts it this way: "For God did not give us a spirit of timidity (of cowardice, of craven and cringing and fawning fear), but [He has given us a spirit] of power and of love and of a calm and well-balanced mind and discipline and self-control."

What the above verse means is that our God is not about 'cringing and fawning' fear. He's not about terror. He is about trust. He doesn't give us Fear. Any time you feel this kind of fear, it is not from God.

What God has done for us is give us weapons to fight this kind of Fear. They include 'power', 'love', and a 'well disciplined mind'. Just as the soldiers of yesterday and today, we have a choice as to what weapons we will use and, even, whether or not we will fight at all. Life will throw things at us. Like it or not, we are in a war zone, even if it is not physical. Satan and Fear and all of those horrible spirits want to take us down. Make no mistake, they hate us. However, we can fight back. God has given us all the tools, all the advanced weaponry we need to take them down. We need to take back what was stolen from us. We need to go on the offensive, right up to the gates of hell, because they will not prevail against God's own.

Ephesians 6:10-18 (Amplified) says, "^{10}In conclusion, be strong in the Lord [be empowered through your union with Him]; draw your strength from Him [that strength which His boundless might provides]." We need to realize that we simply can't do it all by ourselves. We need help and God is more than willing to provide that help. We can be empowered through Him if we let ourselves be. We can draw our strength from Him, if we are willing to 1st: admit we need help and 2nd: surrender control. Remember, God won't do our work for us, but we are also not to try to do everything ourselves either. This is important: We need to be strong IN the Lord. We are meant to work in concert with Him. He did not create us to be mindless, but mindful, mindful of Him. If we keep our focus on Him, He will empower us to do amazing things. In fact, He will empower us to not only defeat Fear, but to occupy that territory that Fear had previously controlled. It isn't enough to defeat Fear just one time, we must occupy that territory so that Fear can never come back.

Here's where the weapons come in: "[11]Put on God's whole armor [the armor of a heavily-armed soldier which God supplies], that you may be able successfully to stand up against [all] the strategies and the deceits of the devil." It doesn't matter what the devil throws at us, with God's whole armor on, we can successfully stand up against ALL the junk the devil tries to throw at us!

We need to understand just what we are fighting: "[12]For we are not wrestling with flesh and blood [contending only with physical opponents], but against the despotisms, against the powers, against [the master spirits who are] the world rulers of this present darkness, against the spirit forces of wickedness in the heavenly (supernatural) sphere." Truly, your boss or co-worker isn't your true enemy. The devil is and God has given us the power to actually win that boss or co-worker. God offers us hope in a hopeless world and the devil hates it.

We need God's armor or we won't make it! "[13]Therefore put on God's complete armor, that you may be able to resist and stand your ground on the evil day [of danger], and, having done all [the crisis demands], to stand [firmly in your place]." Without God's armor on, it's like going into a war zone without a bullet-proof vest.

"[14]Stand therefore [hold your ground], having tightened the belt of truth around your loins and having put on the breastplate of integrity and of moral rectitude and right standing with God...," Here are listed three things with which we can fight. The first thing has to do with our own attitudes: Stand. We need to just stop and look Fear in the face and say, 'No more! In Jesus' name, get out!' This is where the fight begins. It can get a bit rough, but it can also be a lot of fun. Isn't it better on the offensive than the defensive? The second weapon is Truth. God is the truth. Jesus said in John 14:6, "I am the way, the truth, and the life." He also said in John 8:32, "Ye shall know the truth, and the truth shall make you free." I'm sick of being bound by Fear. I want to be free! The truth is I don't have to be afraid anymore. The third weapon is our own integrity. Like it or not, if I am doing something that I know is wrong, God will not honor me. I have to get right. The awesome thing about this is the fact that our own integrity is actually a WEAPON. It protects us!

"[15]And having shod your feet in preparation [to face the enemy with the firm-footed stability, the promptness, and the readiness produced by the good news] of the Gospel of peace." God's peace is a peace that the world simply cannot understand. It is a peace that passes all understanding. God's peace gives us hope in hopeless situations. Then, He does something

45

amazing, unexpected, miraculous even. In the midst of fiery trials, God is there with us. Remember Shadrach, Meshach, and Abednego?

"[16]Lift up over all the [covering] shield of saving faith, upon which you can quench all the flaming missiles of the wicked [one]." No matter how hard Fear tries, he cannot conquer Faith.

"[17]And take the helmet of salvation and the sword that the Spirit wields, which is the Word of God." There are two parts of the armor listed here, the helmet and the sword. The helmet is defensive. If we have that helmet, that knowledge of salvation, on, there is nothing that can hurt us. Fear's primary battlefield is in our own minds. Here is where we decide if we will accept Fear or live by Faith. If we are saved, there is nothing Fear can throw at us that can really do any damage. The sword is our offensive weapon. I don't know about you, but I'd like to do a little bit of damage to my enemy. He hurt me. Isaiah 59:17 says, "For he put on righteousness as a breastplate, and an helmet of salvation upon his head; and he put on the garments of vengeance for clothing, and was clad with zeal as a cloke." This is God speaking here, but He has called us to fight. In fact, He has promised to fight with us and for us. Fear has done damage in our lives. I think it's time for that Fear to be on the run! This Sword that God gives us is very important. It IS God's Word. When we take the time to study the

Bible for ourselves, we get to know God, Himself. When Jesus was tempted by Satan, he used the Bible as His weapon. Satan tried to twist God's Word for his own use, but Jesus knew God's Word thoroughly and was able to turn it back on Satan and defeat him every time! We have that same power given to us.

This last weapon mentioned in this passage is the most important. "[18]Pray at all times (on every occasion, in every season) in the Spirit, with all [manner of] prayer and entreaty. To that end keep alert and watch with strong purpose and perseverance, interceding on behalf of all the saints (God's consecrated people)." Prayer has the power to tear down strongholds. I heard of a woman who, through prayer, was able to take down an entire drug ring, saving countless lives.

I think too often, we underestimate the power of prayer. The amazing thing about prayer, the reason we are commanded to do so, is the fact that it reorients us. Prayer causes us to focus on the Problem-Solver rather than on the problem. Pour out your innermost heart to Jesus. He understands us, utterly. Jesus is not only our creator, He also lived and breathed for over thirty years as a human. He understands our troubles as no one else can. Romans 8:26 says, "Likewise the Spirit also helpeth our infirmities: for we know not what we should pray for as we ought: but the Spirit itself maketh intercession for us with groanings which cannot be uttered." In order to have the victory, we must keep our communications lines open and fully operational. Without constant guidance, we are fighting blind and are more than likely to be blindsided by the enemy of our souls. By walking closely with the Lord and speaking to Him throughout the day, we will be less likely to sustain damage. Certainly, Fear will not stop throwing things at us, but through prayer, it can't hurt us.

Another gift we can be guilty of underestimating is that of praying in tongues. When God baptizes us with His Holy Spirit, we are given the same Spirit Jesus had when He walked the earth. A question a friend of mine asked is quite profound: 'Did Jesus perform miracles as God in the flesh or as flesh filled with (and fully submitted to) the Spirit of God?' If we realize that we have that same Spirit given to us that Jesus used to raise the dead, heal the sick, and cast out demons, we can realize incredible victory in our lives.

When we speak in tongues, our minds rest. This is actually a scientific fact. Recently, I looked up 'speaking in tongues' and 'brain scan' online and found an ABC news article about it on YouTube. According to the doctor who performed the MRI scans on the peoples' brains, the speech portion of the brain is completely at rest when speaking in tongues. This means that when we speak in tongues, we can have that rest, that refreshing, that we so desperately need. Isaiah 28:12 talks about this refreshing that comes from God.

The bottom line in all of this is surrendering our wills and our understanding and obeying and trusting God. When we do that, we are empowered to do mighty things.

There are a few more weapons we have at our disposal: God's Name and the Blood.

God's Name: There is one name that is above every name on heaven or earth and that name is Jesus! When we tell Fear and Satan to get out in Jesus' name, they go. When I start to feel depressed or unworthy or useless or anything else nasty, I speak directly to that feeling and tell it to get out in Jesus' name. It's amazing how that feeling is just suddenly gone! I feel peaceful and good again. Every knee will bow to Jesus' name. I have a friend who was almost attacked by a serial rapist/killer. Before he could touch her, she cried out 'Jesus!' The man was frozen in place, unable to move, until the police came. Indeed, the Name is powerful.

Pleading the Blood: The blood of Jesus covers our sins. It is powerful. When I plead the blood over a situation, there is peace there. I also plead the blood over my family as a kind of shield of protection. We don't know what sort of battles our family members may face in their day. The blood sets up a hedge of protection, a wall around them. The blood also reminds me of just how precious I am to Jesus, that He gave up His life in order to save mine. We don't need to be afraid if we remember Who it is that goes before us, walks with us, and is our rear-guard.

I want to mention one last weapon before going on to the next chapter. That is the weapon of Praise. Habakkuk 3:18 says, "Yet I will rejoice in the Lord, I will joy in the God of my salvation." Remember when I said earlier that attitude can make all the difference in the world? When we choose to praise God, we change our entire outlook. Even in the midst of terrible circumstances, we can choose to rejoice. Philippians 4:4 says, "Rejoice in the Lord always: and again I say, Rejoice." We are actually commanded to rejoice. Paul and Silas were thrown into prison and instead of complaining, they sang praises. The earth shook and their bonds fell off. Praise not only makes you happier, it also brightens others around you. You have power to affect the people in your life for good or ill. Praise and Rejoice and you will have people want to be near you just so they can feel a little better. And, you will get a blessing yourself as well.

In this chapter, we talked about the weapons we have at our disposal to fight Fear. These include the full armor of God, Truth, Righteousness, the

Gospel of Peace, Faith, Salvation, the Sword of the Spirit (or God's Word), Prayer, That Name: Jesus, Pleading the Blood, and finally, Praise. Just as one has to practice in order to get better at shooting an arrow or firing a gun, one needs to practice using these weapons as well. The more you use them, the more formidable you become! In our next chapter, we will discuss the fact that God HEARS us. We are very precious to Him and He is not deaf to our cries. He actually wants us to come to Him with our problems. Read on!

Chapter 5
God Hears You and
He Values You

Psalms 34: 4-10, "I sought the LORD, and he answered me; and he delivered me from all my fears. Those who look to him are radiant; their faces are never covered with shame. This poor man called, and the LORD heard him; he saved him out of all his troubles. The angel of the LORD encamps around those who fear him, and he delivers them. Taste and see that the LORD is good; blessed is the man who takes refuge in him. Fear the LORD, you his saints, for those who fear him lack nothing. The lions may grow weak and hungry, but those who seek the LORD lack no good thing," (NIV).

I love the verses above. I can take those verses as a promise to me. (These promises are for you too, my friends.) I can seek the Lord and He will answer. He may not answer in the way I want Him to, but He will answer me. He will deliver me from all my fears.

Recently, I was privileged to hear a man from Liberia speak, Pastor Edwin Yarsiah Forkpa. He has written a book called *Fourth Man in the Fire* and it is amazing. It is based on his own experiences living in Liberia during their civil war. In that book he talked about the fact that God chose not to deliver him from the fire. Instead, God walked with Pastor Forkpa THROUGH the fire. God, Himself, was that fourth man in the fire. Pastor Forkpa faced a firing squad and lived. In fact, God delivered him not once, but several times from death.

Quoted from the book, "God began to speak to me about the many lost souls trapped by the war [in Liberia]. What if they didn't ever have a chance to go to a church and be saved? What would their fate be? The burden hung over me like a rain cloud." Pastor Forkpa got together with another pastor and started a church right in that town they were all stuck in surrounded by armed men.

He continues, "The devil hadn't succeeded in killing me and now it was my turn. We began walking around in the streets singing and inviting people to the service. Thirty-two people showed up on that porch to have church. Of course there was a much larger audience watching from the street…We sang and preached as the power of God fell. The people were worshiping God, speaking in tongues, and dancing before the Lord."

"God said to me, 'This is why I didn't take you out of the war in the first place. I wanted to use you. All the preachers are gone…I preserved you to be a witness unto me.'"

Pastor Forkpa concludes with, "God's power is not limited to good times. While it is true that God is the Prince of Peace, He also remains the God of war and the Captain of our salvation."

Let's take a look at Psalms 34: 4-10 again.
"I sought the LORD, and he answered me; he delivered me from all my fears." A little child is unafraid and unashamed to ask for help. In fact, little ones expect it, fully trusting their parents to catch them when they fall. Isn't it time we trust the Lord in this way, as well? He is our Father after all.

Verse 5, "Those who look to him are radiant; their faces are never covered with shame." What a wonderful promise, simply by looking to Jesus we can be radiant. There is no shame, ever, in looking to Jesus. He makes our faces glow with love, His love. I know a man who actually died and was given his life back, Rev. Lee Stoneking. He never saw a bright light or Jesus. He said if he had, nothing could have kept him from running with everything he had to Jesus. However, God had other plans for him. God didn't want his life to end just yet. Now, this precious man is completely fearless. If someone comes up to him, waving a gun in his face, his response is, 'Been there, done that! Either way, I win!'

It feels good to walk in victory. God promises us life and life more abundantly (John 10:10). We are not meant to live our lives cowering in fear. We are meant to walk tall and proud. This is what Jesus offers us if we choose to life a life with Him. We can indeed defeat fear forever!

Verse 6, "This poor man called, and the LORD heard him; he saved him out of all his troubles." Understand this: no matter where you are or what you are facing, the Lord will hear you if you call. He will save you, just simply call.

Verse 7, "The angel of the LORD encamps around those who fear him, and he delivers them." This is that 'good fear' we talked about earlier. If we reverence God and live our lives according to His will, He will encamp Himself around us. He will deliver us.

Verse 8, "Taste and see that the LORD is good; blessed is the man who takes refuge in him." Our God is goodness, itself. That is His very nature. In fact, He can't NOT be good. Life with Jesus can be one crazy adventure after another, but it's always good, even when it looks absolutely insane. I heard on the radio that actually achieving goals isn't as satisfying as the 'getting there'. That's what life with Jesus is, LIFE, the incredible wonder of 'getting there'. When we throw in our lot with Jesus, we are blessed beyond our wildest expectations. The verse above says, 'Go ahead and try it out for yourself. You'll see that the Lord is indeed good.'

Verse 9, "Fear the LORD, you his saints, for those who fear him lack nothing." There's that 'good fear' again. And, it comes with yet another promise. 'Those who fear Him lack nothing.' God will always provide our needs, always. Another story found in Pastor Forkpa's book is of a family that was holed up in their home without food and water for several days. Finally, the father prayed and asked God for help. Earlier, he had gotten one of his children a water bed. Not knowing much about them, the father had failed to put the chemicals into the water. They were able to use that water to sustain their lives until it was safe for them to leave their home!

Verse 10, "The lions may grow weak and hungry, but those who seek the LORD lack no good thing." This verse just reiterates the verse above. If we but seek the Lord, He will hear us and provide for us. We really have nothing to fear, not if we're truly seeking Jesus!

The verses above discuss the fact that God hears us. Now, I want to focus on why. Simply put, it is the fact that you, my friend, are very precious to Him.

Matthew 10: 29-31 says, "What's the price of a pet canary? Some loose change, right? And God cares what happens to it even more than you do. He pays even greater attention to you, down to the last detail—even numbering the hairs on your head! So don't be intimidated by all this bully talk. You're worth more than a million canaries," (MSG).

I confess, I've never tried to buy a bird, but every time I've been in a pet shop, I've seen plenty of them for sale. The idea of the verses above is the fact that just as God cares about the smallest, insignificant creatures in this world, He cares a great deal more about you. He even knows how many hairs there are on your very head! My husband jokes that as he gets older, it gets easier and easier for God to count his! However, the point is that God does care. You are indeed very precious to Him. He gave up glory for you and for me.

We've got it pretty cushy here in the United States. For instance, we can choose to go camping for the weekend and then come home to sleep in our nice comfortable beds. I do know of some ladies (and gentlemen too!) who wouldn't dream of 'roughing it' even for a weekend. Their idea of roughing it is sleeping in a hotel room that is less than five stars. Yet Jesus gave up all the glory of heaven, all the adulation and praise of the angels, to come here to live for over thirty years in poverty and then to die a horrible death on a cross. The Bible says He didn't even have a pillow. He did all that for you and me.

Jesus didn't have to do that for us. He could've just destroyed the earth and started over again, but He didn't. He chose to suffer for us. He chose to experience all the evils Satan and the world could throw at Him for our sakes. The thing is He always had the victory. No matter how bad things looked, He never lost the victory. His life is an example to us of what walking in victory looks like. He was never afraid. Yes, He did experience sorrow, but never crippling fear.

Jesus completely submitted His flesh to His Holy Spirit. That is His ultimate secret of success. He always knew the truth. It didn't matter what the world threw at Him, He didn't let it scare Him because He knew what the future held for Him. He even admitted that He didn't want to die a horrible death, but that too He submitted to His Holy Spirit and let it rest there. He didn't hold onto things He wasn't supposed to. Jesus knew He was going to die and He knew how. But, He knew it wouldn't end there. He knew He was going to rise from the dead. He knew that not only was He going to get the ultimate victory, but He would be giving us the opportunity to have the ultimate victory as well.

Galatians 5:22-23 says, "But what happens when we live God's way? He brings gifts into our lives, much the same way that fruit appears in an orchard—things like affection for others, exuberance about life, serenity. We develop willingness to stick with things, a sense of compassion in the heart, and a conviction that a basic holiness permeates things and people. We find ourselves involved in loyal commitments, not needing to force our way in life, able to marshal and direct our energies wisely," (MSG).

The Amplified Bible puts Galatians 5:22-23 this way, "But the fruit of the [Holy] Spirit [the work which His presence within accomplishes] is love, joy (gladness), peace, patience (an even temper, forbearance), kindness, goodness (benevolence), faithfulness, Gentleness (meekness, humility), self-control (self-restraint, continence). Against such things there is no law [that can bring a charge]."

The above verses list, in detail, some of the major things Jesus offers us. The first thing listed is love. Did you know that God is love? That's found in I John 4:8. God loves you. He wants what is best for you. He offers you that love, but you need to accept it. Just as you need to spend time with your spouse in order to truly love and receive love from him or her, you need to spend time with God in order to give and receive His love. Did you also know that love casts out fear?

59

I John 4:18 says, "There is no fear in love; but perfect love casteth out fear: because fear hath torment. He that feareth is not made perfect in love," (KJV). God's love is perfect and that love casts out fear completely. Do you want to be made free from fear and torment? Then, allow God's love to perfect you. You can have the victory over fear, but only if you let God work in you.

God also offers us joy. There is power in rejoicing. How can we be afraid when we are filled with joy? A great example of this truth is found in Acts 16:25-26, "And at midnight Paul and Silas prayed, and sang praises unto God: and the prisoners heard them. And suddenly there was a great earthquake, so that the foundations of the prison were shaken: and immediately all the doors were opened, and everyone's hands were loosed," (KJV). Our praise can shake the very foundations, loose our chains, and make fear run for cover!

God offers us peace. You can't have fear and peace at the same time. It's like trying to have light and darkness in the same space. Not possible. Light wins, always. God's peace wins, always!

God offers us patience. I already discussed some of the experiences of Pastor Forkpa. In this case the bottom line is simply this: You have a choice, walk in God's peace or walk in fear. Which will it be?

God offers us kindness, goodness, and gentleness. I want to be kind and good and gentle. It is so wonderful to draw near to the One who is kind to me, is good to me, and is gentle with me. By His Spirit, I can choose to walk in kindness, goodness, and gentleness. I can completely escape from fear and live in a way that feels good.

God offers us faithfulness. God is always faithful. He never breaks any of His promises to us. He never goes back on His Word. He helps us to be the same way.

God offers us self-control. We can choose how we will behave at any given moment. We can allow the circumstances around us to influence us or not. We can allow our emotions to get the better of us or not. We can walk in fear or not. It is our choice. It is my choice and yours.

In many ways, we need to change our thought patterns and our habits, but it can be done through the power of God's Spirit. We just simply need to walk with Jesus, rather than trying to go at it on our own. If we will walk with Jesus, delight in Him, draw near to Him, He will walk with us. He will direct our paths. He will give us the very desires of our hearts.

Proverbs 3:6 says, "In all thy ways acknowledge Him, and He shall direct thy paths," (KJV). James 4:8 says, "Draw nigh unto God, and He will draw night unto you...," (KJV). Psalm 37:4 says, "Delight thyself also in the Lord, and He shall give thee the desires of thine heart," (KJV). Jesus longs to direct your way and draw near to you and to give you the desires of your heart. Just as parents enjoy giving good things to their children, so also God enjoys giving good things to those who choose to be His.

I like The Message version of Proverbs 3:5-12, "Trust God from the bottom of your heart; don't try to figure out everything on your own. Listen for God's voice in everything you do, everywhere you go; he's the one who will keep you on track. Don't assume that you know it all. Run to God! Run from evil! Your body will glow with health, your very bones will vibrate with life! Honor God with everything you own; give him the first and the best. Your barns will burst, your wine vats will brim over. But don't, dear friend, resent God's discipline; don't sulk under his loving correction. It's the child he loves that GOD corrects; a father's delight is behind all this."

We are so precious to God. In fact, He delights in us. God chose us to be His bride! He loves us that much. He went beyond the extra mile that we might be free from bondage and evil. I heard one day on the radio a lady talking about relationships, vertical and horizontal. Vertical relationships are ones where someone is in authority over someone else, like parents and children, bosses and employees, etc. Horizontal relationships are those which are equal, like co-workers, spouses, etc. God has a vertical relationship with us already. He is God and we are not. However, God wants more than that. He wants to elevate us to a horizontal relationship with Him, as His very bride, sitting on His throne with Him. That, to me, is mind-blowing. The very creator of the universe wants to sit next to me! He also wants to sit next to you. He wants you to rule and reign with Him, starting here and lasting through all eternity. That's love!

A man preached once that a twenty dollar bill would still be worth twenty dollars even if it had mud all over it. The bill itself is merely a piece of paper, with worth assigned to it. God has assigned so much more worth to us. He offers to take the mud off of us and clean us up. He offers us a place next to Him here and now in His kingdom and in the life to come. Do you want that for yourself?

God hears us and He values us. Bad things may happen, but the Bible is very clear on these two points. The question is will we receive what God has for us? It's our choice, every moment of every day.

In the next chapter, we will discuss those things that cause fear. Sometimes, we need to simply recognize those triggers in our lives. If you don't realize it's there, how can you fight it? Know thy enemy and defeat him! Read on!

Chapter 6
Things that Cause Fear and What to Do About It

Sickness, financial troubles, various trials, personal attacks, all these things can cause fear in our lives. What can we do about it? How do we pray?

First of all, we simply must put things into perspective. Jesus was never afraid to talk about Satan or even to speak directly to him. This was because He knew Satan could never defeat Him. No matter what the world or Satan threw, Jesus would always have the ultimate victory and there was nothing the enemy could do about it.

One thing it is important to do is to identify exactly what we fear. For some that will be easy. For others, it is not always so clear. Another way to put it is this: What is holding you back? Sometimes, our fears can be completely emotional, such as fear of failure, fear of success, or fear of looking stupid in front of others. We don't try new things because we're afraid.

Another thing to think about is what is feeding our fear? Sometimes, we need to get rid of pride in our lives. Pride can actually hinder us from getting the help we need or taking the risks necessary to realize our dreams. Pride keeps us blinded to our own faults and hinders our growth. How can we change if we don't acknowledge our need to change? If you or I have a problem saying 'I'm sorry' or 'Can you help me?' pride is at work. If you or I have a problem saying 'You're right and I'm wrong', pride is at work. Get rid of it. Proverbs 16:18 says, "First pride, then the crash—the bigger the ego, the harder the fall," (The MSG).

If we put things in perspective, we can see how silly it is to be prideful about anything. All our lives we've needed help of some kind, whether it was learning to read or simply learning the ropes to our new jobs. We've received help from books, from others, and from the Lord, knowingly or unknowingly. How simple it is to let go of our pride and get the help, insight, and even encouragement we need. It is better to live without crippling fear than holding onto both pride and fear. Pride and fear go hand-in-hand. You can't have one without the other. Of course, Pride says, 'I'm not afraid.' Ha! Don't believe it. Pride is terrified of being found out, because if it is found out, it may be thrown out. Well, good riddance!

Something else that can feed fear and hinder growth in our lives is an unforgiving or bitter attitude. Who haven't you forgiven in your life?

Was it a family member? Was it a friend who deceived you? Was it a boss who treated you unfairly? Don't be afraid to look long and hard into your past and root out that bitterness you've been harboring. It's like a weed that needs to be pulled up by the roots. If unforgiveness or bitterness is not dealt with, it is like a cancer in your life. It is a dream killer and will eat you alive.

Sometimes, we have legitimate reasons for being angry and hurt over things done to us. It may be that some person really did do you wrong. It's okay to acknowledge that. Forgiveness doesn't mean acting like it never happened. Forgiveness is actually 'paying for it yourself'. I know that doesn't make sense. Bear with me and I'll explain. Say you and a friend go out to eat at a restaurant and your friend forgot to bring his wallet. You, being the wonderful person you are pay for the two of you and don't expect your friend to pay you back. You have 'forgiven' your friend's debt. Forgiveness doesn't mean you forget it ever happened. The next time you two go out to eat, you will probably make sure your friend has his wallet with money in it on him.

Forgiveness doesn't mean that now you have to trust that person. For instance, say someone robbed your home. They return your stuff and you forgive them. Now, that doesn't mean that they don't go to jail and it certainly doesn't mean that you will let them house-sit for you! Forgiveness and trust are two totally separate things. When someone hurts you, you don't have to go back and be best friends with that person. What forgiveness does mean is that you won't hold it against them. You let those feelings go. Of course you had a right to be angry, but don't let it end there. Don't hold onto your anger, justified or not. When you hold onto unforgiveness, you let it control you. When you let go of those feelings, they have no power over you anymore.

Keeping things in perspective think of all the rotten things you've done in your life. Jesus forgave you. We are commanded to forgive others. Really, this is for our own benefit more than for the person who wronged you. God wants you to be free. Holding onto bitterness is not freedom, it is bondage.

In some ways, forgiveness needs to become a habit. Some hurts can go so deep, that it has to be untangled like a big knot, one string at a time. Every day, sometimes several times a day, we need to decide to forgive that person. Over time, the knot does get untangled and one day, we find ourselves completely free. This is the life God intends for us. Again, however, it is our choice. Which will you choose, bitterness or forgiveness?

Psalm 73:21-28 says it well, "Then I realized that my heart was bitter, and I was all torn up inside. I was so foolish and ignorant—I must have seemed like a senseless animal to you. Yet I still belong to you; you hold my right hand. You guide me with your counsel, leading me to a glorious destiny. Whom have I in heaven but you? I desire you more than anything on earth. My health may fail, and my spirit may grow weak, but God remains the strength of my heart; he is mine forever. Those who desert him will perish, for you destroy those who abandon you. But as for me, how good it is to be near God! I have made the Sovereign LORD my shelter, and I will tell everyone about the wonderful things you do," (NLT).

Basically, the story behind Psalm 73 is a man was jealous because he worked hard, and all he saw was toil and trouble. The wicked seemed to get on so well. It wasn't fair. However, this man looked and saw their end and it wasn't pretty. He realized that no matter what life threw at him, he had the Lord. I love the last few verses: "When I was beleaguered and bitter, totally consumed by envy, I was totally ignorant, a dumb ox in your very presence. I'm still in your presence, but you've taken my hand. You wisely and tenderly lead me, and then you bless me. You're all I want in heaven! You're all I want on earth! When my skin sags and my bones get brittle, GOD is rock-firm and faithful. Look! Those who left you are falling apart! Deserters, they'll never be heard from again. But I'm in the very presence of GOD—oh, how refreshing it is! I've made Lord GOD my home. GOD, I'm telling the world what you do!" (MSG).

Basically, I was an idiot, but you didn't treat me like one. You tenderly led me and then you blessed me with the truth. I am in the very presence of God. How good that is! We have the opportunity to be in the very presence of God, to make God our home. There is no better life (here or in the life to come) than simply walking with Jesus wherever He leads us.

One more thing I'd like to say before leaving the topics of pride and unforgiveness: You can't have the victory all by yourself.

John Donne said, "No man is an Island, entire of itself; every man is a piece of the Continent, a part of the main; if a clod be washed away by the sea, Europe is the less, as well as if a promontory were, as well as if a manor of thy friends or of thine own were; any man's death diminishes me, because I am involved in Mankind; And therefore never send to know for whom the bell tolls; It tolls for thee."

John Donne got it right in that truly no one can have any kind of life of victory all by himself. A life well lived is lived in community with others.

It's not your job you'll think about on your death bed, but those whose lives have touched you and those whose lives you have touched.

However, I think John Donne did miss one thing. We are all a part of the joys and sorrows of one another, but we are also linked inexorably to our Creator. We were created to worship. God wants us to live in victory, but that is impossible without Him. Now, man has done some pretty amazing things without acknowledging God. Think about the tower of Babel. However, to truly live a victorious, joyful, peaceful, abundant life one must live it with God.

My husband made the statement, "So many people live FOR God, but very few actually walk WITH Him." In order to have the victory in our lives, in order to truly defeat fear forever, we must learn to walk with Jesus. He needs to be a part of every aspect of our lives. He is interested, even in the most mundane things. He cares about you. He wants to be a part of your life.

Think of it this way, God has called us His bride. When two people love each other, they share their lives with one another. They share with each other the things that get them excited or angry or just find interesting. A true love relationship is not just physical. It is also emotional and spiritual. It is a vital, living thing.

It grows and changes over the years. My love for my husband has grown and changed as the years have gone by. I've discovered new things to love and appreciate about him just as he has found in me. In effect, we are Jesus' fiancé. We need to take time to spend with Jesus every day. In fact, God's Word says we should 'acknowledge Him in all our ways.' Proverbs 3:5-6 says, "Trust in the LORD with all thine heart; and lean not unto thine own understanding. In all thy ways acknowledge him, and he shall direct thy paths," (KJV). Remember when I talked about horizontal and vertical relationships? Though the Lord is so much greater than we are, He wants to elevate us to a horizontal relationship with Him, one on one. This simply means we walk WITH Him throughout our days.

How do we walk with God? Well, it's simple really. Just talk to Him throughout the day. Realize He's always there with you. Pray. Ask for help when you don't know what to do. Ask for His opinion on…whatever. Speak in tongues. There's nothing like it in the world for reorienting us when we become frazzled. The more we include the Lord in our lives, the more He will share with us what He is thinking. As we draw near to Him, He draws near to us, (James 4:8).

Now, onto other things that can cause fear and what to do about them: Psalm 23, "God, my shepherd! I don't need a thing. You have bedded me down in lush meadows, you find me quiet pools to drink from. True to your word, you let me catch my breath and send me in the right direction. Even when the way goes through Death Valley, I'm not afraid when you walk at my side. Your trusty shepherd's crook makes me feel secure. You serve me a six-course dinner right in front of my enemies. You revive my drooping head; my cup brims with blessing. Your beauty and love chase after me every day of my life. I'm back home in the house of GOD for the rest of my life," (NLT).

Let's look at these verses in a little more detail. "God, my shepherd! I don't need a thing. You have bedded me down in lush meadows, you find me quiet pools to drink from. True to your word, you let me catch my breath and send me in the right direction," Psalm 23:1-3. Now, sheep are very dependent creatures. They have to be led everywhere and watched carefully, or they'll end up in trouble. When there is trouble, they don't know how to get out of it. Wolves, bears, and lions will hunt them because they are especially vulnerable. Without a good shepherd, the sheep will die.

Like it or not, we humans are a lot like sheep. However, we have a loving Shepherd to care for us, if we choose to follow him. (Remember the part about sheep being led. It's not like herding cattle and forcing them to go in a certain direction. Sheep know their master's voice and FOLLOW him.) It's when we follow our Shepherd closely that we are blessed. We have plenty to eat and drink. We have the rest we need and the direction we crave. We don't need to be afraid, ever, because we are following our Shepherd. He will fight the wolf and bear and lion for us.

Verses 4-5, "Even when the way goes through Death Valley, I'm not afraid when you walk at my side. Your trusty shepherd's crook makes me feel secure. You serve me a six-course dinner right in front of my enemies. You revive my drooping head; my cup brims with blessing." Sometimes, like it or not, we have to walk through Death Valley. The Lord actually leads us through Death Valley, but remember, He is with us all the way, even when it's dark. I don't need to be afraid when I know Jesus is by my side. I can choose to walk through Death Valley with confidence and dignity because I'm walking with Jesus. My husband says, "When Satan comes knocking, I just ask Jesus to answer the door!" When Jesus speaks to Satan and his demons, they flee in terror.

One night my husband was preaching at the Federal Medical Center (prison ministry) in our city to a group of men. One of the prisoners was obviously demon possessed. He had this hideous laugh and he sat in the front row. Well, something rose up inside of my husband that night and he preached Jesus like he had never preached Him before. The man kept moving back a row every time Jesus' name was mentioned. Soon, he was at the back of the room, next to the door. Finally, as he was backing out the door, he said, "You can't make me leave." Then, he ran off down the hall, laughing that hideous laugh. My husband just smiled. Of course the demon didn't want to admit defeat, but he couldn't stand hearing that beautiful Name of Jesus. Mark 16:17 says, "And these signs shall follow them that believe; In My Name (Jesus), they shall cast out devils..." (KJV).

Jesus promises to revive our drooping heads. He offers us that rest which is real rest, rest from stress, peace that passes all understanding. He gives us so many blessings; our cups can hardly hold them. They're up to the very brims of our cups, ready to spill over. Those blessings aren't limited to emotional and spiritual blessings either. He will bless our finances if we ask Him and follow His leading. He will bless our physical bodies too. He loves us with an everlasting love (Jeremiah 31:3). He wants to do us good, not evil, but we have to trust Him.

Verse 6, "Your beauty and love chase after me every day of my life. I'm back home in the house of GOD for the rest of my life." How wonderful that God is willing to 'chase' us. He loves us and wants a relationship with us. It's good to be home with Jesus. Acts 17:28 says, "For in him, we live, and move, and have our being…" (KJV). When we choose to walk with God, we live, really live. We move and have adventures that are amazing. We have our very being, we are new creatures, able to accomplish more than we ever thought possible, in (and with) Him. Remember, He doesn't do our work for us, He goes WITH us, always, but it is our choice.

Now for a game plan. What are some strategies to defeating fear now and keeping it out of our lives for good? The obvious first thing to do is repent of your sins (say you're sorry for all the bad things you've done), get baptized in Jesus' name, and receive the Holy Ghost with the evidence of speaking in other tongues, Acts 2:38. That's the whole born again experience, just as Jesus said to Nicodemus in John 3:5, "Jesus answered, Verily, verily, I say unto thee, Except a man be born of water and of the Spirit, he cannot enter into the kingdom of God," (KJV).

However, this is only the beginning. Even after we've repented of our sins, we still occasionally fail. Those books that come after the book of Acts in the Bible were written to churches, people who were already 'saved'. They were still told to repent. It's very simple, really. When you mess up, fess up. Then, don't do it again. If you take a look at those churches, they were pretty messed up. Again, God doesn't do our work for us. He works in us and with us. Pastor Forkpa says, "God isn't interested in good people, He's interested in BETTER people." God doesn't want to just give you miracles in your life; He wants you to BE the miracle.

So, after the initial salvation experience, how can we defeat fear forever? Well, that 'born again' experience is the beginning, but only the beginning. Once a person has been saved, he/she needs to take steps that will insure he/she stays saved. Again, it's really rather simple. Say you were drowning in a lake and someone came along and saved your life. You're not going to run out and jump in that lake again, right? You're going to take swimming lessons, wear a life jacket, be mindful of the weather, etc. You're going to take steps to insure you don't have that terrible experience again. Spiritual salvation is the same. We have been saved from our sins; however, we need to learn how to live a life that is different from what we had been doing before, (because, obviously, what we were doing before wasn't working). We need to learn new ways to talk, to walk, to listen (to others and the Lord).

Think of it this way, when you were saved, you were no longer dead in your sins. You became a brand new creature. II Corinthians 5:17 says, "Therefore if any person is [engrafted] in Christ (the Messiah) he is a new creation (a new creature altogether); the old [previous moral and spiritual condition] has passed away. Behold, the fresh and new has come!" (Amplified). Spiritually, you are no longer a caterpillar, you are now a butterfly. Butterflies are as different from caterpillars as bicycles are from planes, as dogs are from birds. Butterflies look different, they eat differently, they move differently. Can you imagine a butterfly trying to go back to his way of life as a caterpillar? Yet, that is exactly what many people do spiritually.

In this chapter, we looked at some things that can cause fear, such as sickness, financial difficulties, etc. We also looked at some things that might be surprising, yet still can cause fear, such as pride and unforgiveness. We discussed ways of dealing with those things. In the next chapter, we're going to go much more deeply into what to do about that fear. We're going to discuss a changed mindset and how you can have that for yourself. We're going to talk about how you can be your very own miracle to yourself, not by yourself, but most definitely to yourself. I don't know about you, but I'm really excited about this next one! Read on!

Chapter 7
New Creature
New Life
New (Victorious) Habits

I John 3:1a says, "Behold, what manner of love the Father hath bestowed upon us, that we should be called the sons of God," (KJV).

I know I've talked about this a lot, but that's because it is so important. God loves you! I mean, He really loves you.

Titus 3:5-6 says, "Not by works of righteousness which we have done, but according to his mercy he saved us, by the washing of regeneration, and renewing of the Holy Ghost; which he shed on us abundantly through Jesus Christ our Savior," (KJV).

Remember my analogy of the caterpillar versus the butterfly? When we are first saved, we are indeed new creatures. Now, unlike butterflies who instinctively know how to fly, we need to learn. That doesn't mean God hasn't given us wings. We simply need to learn how to use them. The butterfly's life isn't any easier than ours is. First off, he has to get out of his chrysalis. That's hard work and if anyone tries to help him, he'll die. Then, he has to spread his wings out to their full breadth and let them dry. When he first comes out of that chrysalis, his wings are all crumpled up and his body is distended, full of fluid. As he beats his wings up and down, the fluid flows out of his abdomen and into his wings, enabling him to fly. Finally, he's ready to go. Even then, however, he still needs to be wary of danger.

It's the same with us. We need to work hard to stay away from our old habits. Eat them up, completely destroy them. If you have a problem with alcohol, don't go out of your way to walk past a bar! In fact, go out of your way to avoid walking past that bar.

God has filled our spiritual abdomens with rivers of living water. That's the Holy Ghost. We don't want to remain distended and useless. We need to beat our spiritual wings and let those rivers flow in our lives, enabling us to fly. The more we beat our wings, the more that river flows. That river flowing will not only change your life, but it will also affect those around you. Don't be afraid to work hard, be afraid of missing out because you didn't!

After he has learned how to fly, one of the first things a butterfly does is EAT! He finds himself a nice flower and drinks his fill. We, like the butterfly, need to eat too, not just physical food, but Spiritual food, the food of God's Word, the Bible. Take time to read God's Word every day. It will change you and make you better. Don't stop there, though. Apply God's Word to your life. Talk to Him as you read. Ask Him what He's trying to teach you through this passage. It's His love letter to you. Of course, He wants to talk to you about it!

I like to start my day with prayer and Bible reading. It reminds me that I'm not in this crazy life alone. I have divine help. I've quoted from several different versions of the Bible in this book. I recommend that you try all of them. There are several free versions on the Internet. Download and go! E-sword is really good. (Google it.) That is in the King James Version and has a direct translation straight from the Hebrew or Greek of almost every word. There's also a search function. Best of all, it's free! Another great resource for Bibles is BibleGateway.com. You can't download that, but you can look up any passage of Scripture in several versions as well as several languages. Bottom line: take the time to read God's Word— every day. You won't regret it.

Now, back to our butterfly…

Finally, the butterfly has been given a variety of defense mechanisms. Some butterflies have coloring that looks like giant eyes to scare off their enemies. Others have coloring that warn that they would be poisonous to eat. Or, their particular coloring blends in with their surroundings (hide). There is also the obvious defense mechanism, i.e. flight.

It is the same in our lives. We also have been given a variety of defense mechanisms. God has given us a great big sword (There's that Bible again!) to scare off our enemies. When you take the time to not only memorize Scripture, but truly absorb it and implement it in your life, your sword just gets sharper.

My husband owns his own violin business. One of the aspects of his business is repairing instruments. This requires very special, extremely sharp knives. Occasionally, those knives need to be re-sharpened. He has special stones that he uses for this purpose. He knows his knives are sharp enough when he can cut the hair on his arm with practically no effort.

In our own lives, we need to take the time to sharpen our spiritual swords. We do this by spending time every day reading God's Word (the Bible). We need to memorize Scripture. Copy and post them around your house; tape some to your mirror or put them on little cards for you to read while you sit in traffic. There are also CDs with Scripture on them for those aural learners among us. Simply the act of copying

Scripture helps as well. Then, use it in your daily life. Talk to your spouse about what you read that day. Tell your children what God showed you this morning in Scripture. Talk to God about His Word. He loves sharing that with you. He will open up your understanding if you ask Him. James 1:5 says, "If you need wisdom, ask our generous God, and he will give it to you. He will not rebuke you for asking," (NLT).

Another interesting defense mechanism that we can share with a butterfly is his beautiful coloring. Some butterflies have what looks like big eyes on their wings, pretty scary. Other butterflies' coloring tells predators they are poisonous to eat. We, by the way we dress and carry ourselves, act as a witness to both the physical and the spiritual world. As a woman, I (and my daughters) dress modestly, no low cut blouses and no pants, only skirts (below the knee). To some that might seem a bit excessive or restrictive. However, I have found incredible freedom in doing this. To the world, my clothing says, 'I'm a lady. Treat me with dignity and respect.' When people speak to me, they aren't only interested in 'the view'; they are interested in my 'point of view'. My daughters and I have never been limited because of skirts. In fact, they can climb trees just as fast, if not faster, than their brothers! (Just so you know: my husband and sons also dress modestly. They don't go out in public without shirts on. They always have sleeves on their shirts, no tank tops, and they wear pants only, no shorts.) This is something that you have to seek the Lord about yourself. He will lead you and guide you in this issue. Of course your clothes are important to Him. He made the first clothing for people to wear! And yes, it was modest for both the man and the woman. God loves you and wants your best. The world doesn't care at all about you. In fact, it sees you as nothing more than a commodity. Have you noticed how sexy clothing is for little girls nowadays? What's with that?!

Another way to let my enemies know to beware I'm armed and dangerous is the fact that I don't wear jewelry or make-up. The world says if you're a woman, you aren't beautiful without jewelry and make-up. I have taken a stand against that! Many precious ladies won't even check their mail without their 'faces' on! My God says that I am fearfully and wonderfully made in His very image. It doesn't get more beautiful than that! Why follow the world's ideas of beauty? Be a trend setter, not a trend follower. Walk with confidence, knowing that you are not walking alone. Don't be afraid to show the world the real you, beautiful, just the way you are. You don't need help to be beautiful. You already are! You aren't for sale. You are beyond price!

Another defense mechanism we have is simply hiding. Psalm 17:8-9 says, "Keep your eye on me; hide me under your cool wing feathers from the wicked who are out to get me, from mortal enemies closing in," (MSG). Sometimes, the best thing in the world we can do is spiritually 'hide' ourselves. We do that through prayer, speaking in tongues, and simply focusing our minds on Jesus.

The last defense mechanism for the butterfly is simply this: flight. I Timothy 6:11-12 says, "But you, Timothy, man of God: Run for your life from all this [sin]. Pursue a righteous life—a life of wonder, faith, love, steadiness, courtesy. Run hard and fast in the faith. Seize the eternal life, the life you were called to, the life you so fervently embraced in the presence of so many witnesses," (MSG).

Run away from sin and things which pull you down. Run toward life, Jesus, and righteous living. Don't submit yourself to your feelings. Make your feelings submit to Jesus! One of the themes in today's world is 'follow your heart'. That's terrible advice! Don't follow your heart, it's an awful compass. Sometimes, often times, your heart (or your feelings) is just plain wrong. Instead of 'following your heart', follow Jesus, and not reluctantly. Follow Him with fervency. Chase Him with everything you've got. I guarantee that He will lead you into the most wonderful, amazing, fulfilling life adventure beyond your imagination.

James 4:7-10 says, "So let God work his will in you. Yell a loud no to the Devil and watch him scamper. Say a quiet yes to God and he'll be there in no time. Quit dabbling in sin. Purify your inner life. Quit playing the field. Hit bottom, and cry your eyes out. The fun and games are over. Get serious, really serious. Get down on your knees before the Master; it's the only way you'll get on your feet," (MSG). If you want to fly, you must start on your knees before Jesus.

New habits take time. You need to give yourself permission to fail, but don't stay there. So far, we've discussed the fact that if you have followed God's Word as stated by Peter in Acts 2:38 (repentance, baptism in Jesus' name, and being filled with the Holy Ghost with the evidence of speaking in tongues), you are a new creature in Jesus. We've compared that to the differences between life as a caterpillar and life as a butterfly. Now, I want to talk about developing a habit that not only will get you the victory, but help you to keep it forever.

That habit is the habit of praise. Philippians 4:4-9 says, "Celebrate God all day, every day. I mean, revel in him! Make it as clear as you can to all you meet that you're on their side, working with them and not against them. Help them see that the Master is about to arrive. He could show up any minute! Don't fret or worry. Instead of worrying, pray. Let petitions and praises shape your worries into prayers, letting God know your concerns. Before you know it, a sense of God's wholeness, everything coming together for good, will come and settle you down. It's wonderful what happens when Christ displaces worry at the center of your life. Summing it all up, friends, I'd say you'll do best by filling your minds and meditating on things true, noble, reputable, authentic, compelling, gracious—the best, not the worst; the beautiful, not the ugly; things to praise, not things to curse. Put into practice what you learned from me, what you heard and saw and realized. Do that, and God, who makes everything work together, will work you into his most excellent harmonies," (MSG).

In the above verses, we see that we are commanded to celebrate God all day, every day. When you greet the day with praise and worship and a simple smile on your face, it alters everyone and everything around you. People will want to be around you simply because they feel good around you. My father said once, that you will find what you are looking for in your life. If you look for the bad, you will find it. However, if you look for things to rejoice about, you will find that as well. This applies to people also. If you look for the negative in people, you'll be sure to find it. On the other hand, if you look for the good in the people around you, you will find that too.

Carlton Myers says, "Happiness and joy are not the same. Happiness is determined by the happenings, events, and circumstances of life. Joy is determined by the fullness of the Holy Spirit in our lives. So it is possible to be joyful even though you are unhappy. The fullness of the Holy Spirit in us is determined by how much we have surrendered our wills to God. It is also determined by how much of God's Word is in us. Happiness is something you find by searching for it. It is a by-product of losing yourself in serving God and others. The same is true of joy. You cannot work it up. It is a supernatural result of God's spirit."

Like many things in this life, joy is a choice. It doesn't matter what our circumstances are or what is going on around us, we can still choose to rejoice. We have what the world wants so desperately, hope. We need to make it a habit to think on that—constantly.

Another habit that will make a huge difference is that of remembering past victories. My pastor described it as taking down trophies from your mental shelf and occasionally polishing them, taking the time to remember God's priceless, constant presence in our lives.

Part of Israel's problem in the Old Testament was that they did not remember past victories God had given them. They dwelt so much in the present, they forgot all the incredible things God had done for them in even the recent past, such as parting the Red Sea, giving them manna to eat, causing water to pour out of a rock in the desert, and giving them the victory in impossible battles. If Israel had only taken the time to remind each other of all of those miracles and praised the Lord, they probably wouldn't have had to wander around in the dessert for forty years!

Why is it so easy for us, in the emotion of the moment, to forget about past victories? Just because I feel bad now, doesn't mean it was always this way. And, it certainly doesn't mean things will stay this way! We seem to have no problems remembering past hurts or offenses but past victories are something else altogether. Take a few moments, right now, to remember some past victories in your own life. Write them down and remember. Victories can be small or large, such as a time when you chose to ignore your hurt to help someone else. Or simply remember a time when you helped someone else. That's a victory. Remember when you finally realized you needed help and repented of all the bad things you had done. Remember when you were baptized in Jesus' beautiful name. Remember when Jesus first filled you with His Holy Spirit. These are all incredible victories. Victories don't have to be large to be considered important. All victories are important, because they are yours and Jesus'. A victory might be as simple as paying your bills on time or choosing not to spend money on that particular item you thought you wanted. The important thing here is to make it a habit to remember past victories and then praise the Lord for them. You could do it once a week or even every day. The important thing is to do it. Don't forget to praise the Lord for those victories, because, like it or not, we can't have victory without Him. Think of it this way: isn't it more fun to share the victory with someone anyway? You and Jesus can enjoy that victory together. That's the best way and it makes your victories even sweeter.

Now that you've taken the time to remember some of your past victories, I want you to take a little time to remember some past failures. Ooh. Not so fun. However, I don't want you to stay there. I simply want you to remember those times and learn from them. Then, I want you to take some more time and praise the Lord. 'Praise the Lord for my failures?' you ask. Not quite. Rather, praise the Lord in your failures. You weren't alone, not for a moment. Jesus was right with you the whole time. Yes, you failed, but if you asked Him to forgive you, He forgave you. I John 1:9 says, "But if we confess our sins to him, he is faithful and just to forgive us our sins and to cleanse us from all wickedness," (NLT). Satan is notorious for reminding us of our past failures. We need to remember this verse and realize God doesn't lie. Not only does God forgive us of our sins, He helps us to change into better people. When Satan reminds you of your past, quote this Bible verse and tell him to get lost in Jesus' name! He'll run.

When we feel bad because of our sins, that is conviction. God wants us to be right with Him and right with the people around us. Therefore, He convicts us of our sins to help us turn around (repent). If you are still plagued by your sin after you have repented, check to see that you have done all you could to make things right. Do you need to apologize to someone? Do you need to ask for forgiveness? Pride is a funny thing. For some reason, it's not so difficult to say 'I'm sorry', but it can be tremendously difficult to say 'Will you forgive me?' Once you have done all you could to make things right, and you still feel 'bad', that's condemnation. That's of the devil. When we feel condemned, we need to simply reject that feeling, because it's a lie. What I do is this: I say, 'In Jesus' name, condemnation get out!' Instantly, I feel better. If I don't feel better, I say it again until I do. Never underestimate the power of Jesus' name. Demons will flee, but we are in a battle. Some battles are harder than others. Sometimes, you have to simply stand and keep at it. Never forget, John 8:32, "And you will know the truth, and the truth will set you free," (NLT). Your feelings will NOT set you free.

Did you know that in the Hebrew Bible the book of Job is after the book of Psalms? Recently, I was privileged to hear Dr. Daniel Segraves speak at our state's annual United Pentecostal Family Camp Meeting here in Minnesota. Dr. Segraves explained that when we got our version of the Bible, it was from a Greek translation, with a Greek order. I have no idea why the Greeks switched things around, but when you take a look at the Hebrew order, it's quite fascinating. The book of Psalms is a book of songs of praise to God. The theme of the last few chapters of Psalms is 'Praise ye the Lord'. You'll see it over and over again. Having the book of Job follow the book of Psalms is an interesting order.

Job was a righteous man whom God recognized especially. God allowed Satan to do all kinds of terrible things to him to show that Job worshipped God not simply because he was blessed with wealth and happy times, but because he genuinely loved God. Job endured tremendous misfortune at Satan's hand, loss of his wealth, his children, and even his health. Yet, in all of this, he refused to curse God. Instead, "Then Job arose, and rent his mantle, and shaved his head, and fell down upon the ground, and worshipped. And said, naked came I out of my mother's womb, and naked shall I return thither: the Lord gave, and the Lord hath taken away; blessed be the name of the LORD," Job 1:20-21 (KJV).

Joy Haney says in her book, *Women of the Spirit Bible Study, Vol. VI: The Power of Praise*, "Praise is not based on the emotions of a woman, but upon the object of praise, which is God...God is perfect, glorious, mighty, compassionate, and kind. He has done no wrong. Why should He be derived of praise because of our predicament or problem? The bigger the problem, the bigger the praise should be."

Hannah was a beautiful lady. (You can read about her in I Samuel.) She couldn't have children and was devastated because of it. Her sorrow was made even worse by the taunts of her husband's second wife who had several children. So, Hannah went into the temple and prayed desperately for a child. She told God that she would dedicate that child to Him, if only she could conceive.

Well, time passed and she had a little boy. She called him Samuel. She loved him and cared for him until he was old enough to serve in the temple. Then, keeping her word to the Lord, she brought him there. She was only able to visit him once a year. (It was several days journey from her home to the temple.)

On the day Hannah left her little boy in the temple, she prayed this, "My heart rejoiceth in the Lord, mine horn is exalted in the Lord: my mouth is enlarged over mine enemies; because I rejoice in thy salvation. There is none holy as the Lord: for there is none beside thee: neither is there any rock like our God…He raiseth up the beggar from the dunghill, to set them among princes, and to make them inherit the throne of glory: for the pillars of the earth are the Lord's and He hath set the world upon them. He will keep the feet of his saints, and the wicked shall be silent in darkness; for by strength shall no man prevail. The adversaries of the Lord shall be broken to pieces; out of heaven shall He thunder upon them: the Lord shall judge the ends of the earth; and He shall give strength unto His king, and exalt the horn of His anointed," I Samuel 2:1-2, 8-10 (KJV).

Because Hannah chose to praise God and keep her word, she was given a mighty prophecy. Her son became one of the greatest prophets in history. He anointed kings and walked closely with God. I think it's because of what Hannah put into him while he was still a little boy living at home. Hannah taught him to love God above all others. It couldn't have been easy for her to say good-bye to her son, but she trusted God to care for him. She had taught him well and he was ready for what God had for him. (By the way, God gave Hannah other children as well.)

The bottom line is, it doesn't matter what is going on in our lives, we need to praise the Lord anyway. Hebrews 13:13-15 says, "So let's go outside, where Jesus is, where the action is—not trying to be privileged insiders, but taking our share in the abuse of Jesus. This "insider world" is not our home. We have our eyes peeled for the City about to come. Let's take our place outside with Jesus, no longer pouring out the sacrificial blood of animals but pouring out sacrificial praises from our lips to God in Jesus' name," (MSG).

We have been given so much. We don't have to sacrifice animals to atone for our wickedness anymore. Instead we are to bring sacrifices of praise. That means we praise the Lord when we fail miserably, because He forgives our sin if we ask Him. We are to praise God continually, no matter how we feel or what our circumstances are. Now, that does not mean that we ignore tragedies in our lives. It simply means that we praise the Lord anyway. God knows what we are going through and He goes with us. Praising God does not give Him more power. He already has all power. The power of praise is in helping us to realize that significant fact. When we take the time to praise God, all of our little complaints fade away. We are shown the truth and the truth sets us free—to live the way God intended us to live—victoriously!

In this chapter, we discussed what it means to be a new creature and new habits we need to cultivate in order to not only get the victory, but to keep it. In the next chapter, we're going to discuss being confident of our victory and growing in our walk with Jesus. I don't want to just live and work for Jesus; I want to walk, daily, moment by moment, WITH Him. Read on!

Chapter 8
Learning to Walk WITH Jesus Confident of Our Victory

What We Have In Christ:
A love that can never be fathomed;
A life that can never die;
A righteousness that can never be tarnished;
A peace that can never be understood;
A rest that can never be disturbed;
A joy that can never be diminished;
A hope that can never be disappointed;
A glory that can never be clouded;
A light that can never be darkened;
A happiness that can never be interrupted;
A strength that can never be enfeebled;
A purity that can never be defiled;
A beauty that can never be marred;
A wisdom that can never be baffled;
Resources that can never be exhausted. --Author Unknown.

Take a few moments to read the above poem through again. It's worth dwelling on. I've been thinking about just the first line for the past several days. Jesus' love for us is truly unfathomable, that He would spend over 6000 years sending prophets and putting into place the perfect time for His personal appearance here on Earth to die for us and then raise Himself up again is unbelievable. The very fact that He was willing to take on sinful flesh for our sakes still amazes me. Then, He kept that flesh. He still wears that flesh and rules, not as an incredibly large being, but as flesh, like me.

I talked back in chapter 5 about the fact that God wants to sit next to me. In fact, He wants me to sit on His throne—next to Him! That kind of love is more than I can even understand. I pray that I may learn to love Him more, to show it in my daily life, to respond to His love, rather than just take it for granted.

The rest of the poem is also worth dwelling on, life everlasting, untarnished righteousness and peace that passes all human understanding. Jesus doesn't just offer me hope in the life to come, He offers me eternal life, LIFE, starting right now. That righteousness the author talks about is not my own. It's His and can't be dirtied by this world. I don't have to work so hard to be righteous ON MY OWN. I can receive His help and truly become more like Him. That's where that peace comes in. My hope isn't in my own skill or talents, it's in Him. It's ALL in Him.

Of course, the poem goes on to list more that we have in Jesus. The thing is, if you sat down, I bet you could list even more than the 'unknown author' did. The question for you (and me too!) is this: What kind of a difference is this knowledge about what we have in Christ going to make in our everyday lives? If we simply read it and think, 'Hey that's cool,' then go on our merry way, it means very little. However, if we read and apply, our lives will be changed. How much more will reading and applying God's very Word to our lives make a difference!

"Being confident of this very thing, that he which hath begun a good work in you will perform it until the day of Jesus Christ," Philippians 1:6 (KJV). Remember what Pastor Forkpa said, 'God isn't interested in good people; He's interested in BETTER people.' When we are first saved, that's not the end. Repenting of our sins, being baptized in Jesus' beautiful name, and being filled with His incredible Holy Spirit is not the end all for our salvation. It is only the beginning. Just as a newborn baby is expected to grow and mature and eventually live a life of his or her own, so we are expected to grow and mature—spiritually.

Let's go back to the caterpillar versus the butterfly example. A caterpillar has teeth (or rather mandibles, i.e. insect teeth) so he can munch on leaves. A butterfly on the other hand, does not have teeth. Instead he has a proboscis that curls up into his mouth and unfurls into a flower allowing him to 'suck' out the nectar. It functions like a straw. The point I'm trying to make here is this: can you imagine a butterfly trying to suck on a leaf? Or worse, trying to crawl around as if he didn't have wings? It's rather crazy, but that is what many Christians do. Though they are saved from their old life, though they are new creatures, they act as if nothing has changed. The scary thing is, just as a butterfly trying to suck on a leaf would soon die of starvation, so does the Christian who doesn't get spiritual food.

With babies, it is either grow or die. If babies don't eat, they die. It is the same with butterflies and Christians. Ephesians 1:17-18 says, "That the God of our Lord Jesus Christ, the Father of glory, give unto me, the spirit of wisdom and revelation in the knowledge of him. That the eyes of my understanding be enlightened; that I may know what is the hope of his calling, and what the riches of the glory of his inheritance in the saints." God has for us a banquet of spiritual food that we might grow in knowledge and wisdom and understanding. As we grow in our knowledge of Jesus, our fears become less and less. We realize just how mighty He is.

"That You would grant me, according to the riches of Your glory, to be strengthened with might by Your Spirit in the inner man; that Christ may dwell in my heart by faith; so that I can be rooted and grounded in love, that I may be able to comprehend with all saints what is the breadth, and length, and depth, and height: and to know the love of Christ, which passeth knowledge, that I might be filled with all the fullness of God," Ephesians 3:16-19. This is part of a prayer that Paul prayed, but it's for us as well. We too can be strengthened with might. We can be strong and unafraid because of God's Spirit in us, in our inner man. The more we fill our hearts and minds with Jesus, the more He dwells in our hearts and minds. Our faith grows and our fear shrinks. That's what it means to be 'rooted and grounded in love'. What do we fill our hearts with? Do we make God a priority in our lives?

The children have a song that goes something like this:
Read your Bible and Pray every day and you'll grow, grow, grow,
And you'll grow, grow, grow, and you'll grow, grow, grow.
Read your Bible and Pray every day and you'll grow, grow, grow.
Don't read your Bible and don't Pray every day and you'll shrink, shrink, shrink,
And you'll shrink, shrink, shrink, and you'll shrink, shrink, shrink.
Don't read your Bible and don't Pray every day and you'll shrink, shrink, shrink.

Although the song is simple and cute, it contains a profound truth. In order to grow, in order to survive, we need to read our Bible and Pray

EVERY day. If you don't have it in your schedule for the day, put it in. Like it or not, we are in a war. Satan will not take a vacation. We cannot afford to. Our very survival is at stake. Satan wants to hurt Jesus and the only way he can do that is by hurting us. The battle isn't between Satan and Jesus, it's between Satan and us. Now, Jesus is certainly not just a spectator in this war. He gave His life, remember? Jesus has given us all the power we need to defeat the enemy of our souls. Make no mistake, we don't get to remove ourselves from this battle. That is simply not an option. We must fight and we must grow. For if we do, if we grow in wisdom and understanding in Jesus, if we fight the good fight, we WILL win.

Psalm 138:8 says, "The Lord will perfect that which concerneth me: thy mercy, O Lord, endureth for ever: forsake not the works of thine own hands." God isn't finished with me or you yet. He has a wonderful tapestry in mind for your life that is beautiful beyond your wildest dreams. He is making YOU beautiful beyond your wildest dreams. Submit to Him and He will bless you.

Psalm 139:1-4, "O Lord, thou has searched me, and known me. Thou knowest my downsitting and mine uprising, thou understandest my thought afar off. Thou compassest my path and my lying down, and art acquainted with all my ways. For there is not a word in my tongue, but, lo, O Lord, thou knowest it altogether." We can't hide anything from Jesus. He already knows our past, our present, and our future. He knows the mistakes we have made and He knows the problems we face. He knows all about our good attitudes and our not so good attitudes. Yet, for all of that, He loves us and He offers us a chance to grow and change, just like our friend the butterfly. He had a pretty dramatic change from a leaf-chewing-ground-crawler to a nectar-drinking-flying-work-of-art. God wants to give us wings as well. We just need to submit and get ourselves enrolled in flight school!

Psalm 19:11-14 "There's more: God's Word warns us of danger and directs us to hidden treasure. Otherwise how will we find our way? Or know when we play the fool? Clean the slate, God, so we can start the day fresh! Keep me from stupid sins, from thinking I can take over your work; then I can start this day sun-washed, scrubbed clean of the grime of sin. These are the words in my mouth; these are what I chew on and pray. Accept them when I place them on the morning altar, O God, my Altar-Rock, God, Priest-of-My-Altar," (MSG).

In order to do well in flight school, we must study the manual. The manual directs us in how our instruments work and what to do in case of danger. It is the same with the Bible. The Bible directs us in how we were meant to live and move and have our being—in Jesus! The Bible teaches us how to walk, talk, and even think. We were made to soar through the air, not crawl around on the ground. We were made to drink nectar from beautiful flowers, not chew (or suck) on leaves. When we follow God's plans, God's manual for our lives, we learn to soar. We become what we were meant to be. We find that joy that is unfathomable, that peace that nothing can touch.

However, it isn't enough to merely study the manual. It isn't enough to just read the Bible. We need to apply it to our lives. For instance, when it came time to potty train my oldest daughter, I read a lot of books about it. However, she didn't learn to use the potty by herself until I actually applied what I had learned. We cannot experience change in our lives unless we actually change something in our lives. We need to actually DO some flying. Studying that flight manual might be a lot of fun, but it's not useful until you apply it and get off the ground!

Psalm 19 also talks about 'stupid' sins. The New Living Translation (NLT) calls them 'deliberate' sins, Amplified (AMP) and the King James Version (KJV) translates it as 'presumptuous' sins, and the New International Version (NIV) calls them 'willful' sins. The point is we need to be kept from doing those things that we know are wrong. To yell at someone and curse them because they cut us off in traffic is wrong. It's just sin. To lie or steal or break any of the Ten Commandments is sin. But, we have power over sin if we have Jesus. When He fills us with His Holy Spirit, we are given the power to choose to not sin anymore. And, if we do fail, if we do sin, we don't lose that power. All we have to do is get up, fess up, ask for forgiveness, and don't do it again. The Bible says resist Satan and he will flee.

"So let God work his will in you. Yell a loud no to the Devil and watch him scamper. Say a quiet yes to God and he'll be there in no time. Quit dabbling in sin. Purify your inner life. Quit playing the field. Hit bottom, and cry your eyes out. The fun and games are over. Get serious, really serious. Get down on your knees before the Master; it's the only way you'll get on your feet," James 4:7-10 (MSG). "So humble yourselves before God. Resist the devil, and he will flee from you," James 4:7 (NLT). Sometimes, it's not fun to submit to God, but it's good. Remember, God wants to bless you, to grow you up, and to make you a miracle to yourself. Sometimes, that requires impossible situations and difficult circumstances. When you are in the middle of a storm, it's hard to remember the sunshine before. However, when the storm ends, the grass is greener, the sky bluer, and the air sweeter. It feels good to overcome!

Psalm 18:32-33, "God arms me with strength, and he makes my way perfect," (NLT). "He makes my feet like hinds' feet [able to stand firmly or make progress on the dangerous heights of testing and trouble]; He sets me securely upon my high places," (AMP). It is our Lord who will strengthen us. He leads us in ways that are perfect and sure. We can trust that He knows what He's doing in our lives. He makes our feet to be able to stand firm in the midst of danger, testing, and troubles. He makes us secure and even allows us to look down at the breathtaking view from the heights of mountains!

I was being a little poetic there, but stay with me. I enjoy sitting in the window seat of an airplane because of the spectacular view. The world just looks different from above. I wish I could be an astronaut and see the earth from space. The pictures I've seen are simply breathtaking. This, spiritually, is what the Lord offers us. He allows us to take a moment or more and view our lives from the heights and our perspective changes. That, in many ways, is what the Lord is all about with us. When we view things from God's perspective and look at our world through Jesus' eyes, our perspective changes. We begin to see that difficult co-worker with compassion, realizing that his/her life is just as difficult, if not more so, than ours. At the very least, we have a hope that they do not.

Think about it. Is your perspective the same as when you were a child? Of course not. You know it's a really bad idea to eat only candy and nothing nutritious, right? At the very least, you'll end up feeling very sick.

Think about some of the wisest people you know. Jesus offers you His mind. You can be wise and mature as well. Children end up in trouble because they don't think about the consequences of things. When we mature in Christ, not only does our understanding change, but we can see things that others cannot, because our perspective is different. God gives us wisdom, not man's wisdom which is faulty, but His wisdom which is perfect.

We have the mind of Christ, which is pure, peaceful, and true. Part of the reason Jesus became a man and walked the earth was to show us how to live in purity and truth. Jesus, as a man, had to contend with temptation, just as we do. He had to contend with fear, betrayal, and death on a cross. This He knew in advance. Yet, still He submitted His unwilling flesh to His perfect Spirit. Then, and only then, did He have the strength to sacrifice His life in such a horrific way for our sakes.

I think sometimes we are tempted to beat ourselves up when we don't know what the right choice is. We think because we have the mind of Christ, we should just automatically know. That isn't always the case. Frankly, there's no faith needed if we already know the future. Just as a teen-ager needs the opportunity to try new things and fail, we need to give ourselves that same opportunity. God does. He doesn't fault us just because we can't do something. Just because it may take awhile to learn to play an instrument doesn't make me stupid. It's something new. Sometimes, we simply need to just trust God to lead us one step at a time. That can be very exciting indeed!

How does one mature in Christ? Well, it's actually not at all difficult. First, realize where you've come from (and praise God that you are not there anymore). Then, figure out where you are now. Finally, decide where you want to go. Seek the Lord for His guidance in your life and ask Him what He wants for you. Tell Him the desires of your heart. Share your heart with Him and ask Him to share His heart with you. As you take the time to draw nearer to Him, He will draw nearer to you. As you seek Him with all your heart, He will give you your heart's desires.

Philippians 4:8 says, "Finally, brethren, whatsoever things are true, whatsoever things are honest, whatsoever things are just, whatsoever things are pure, whatsoever things are lovely, whatsoever things are of good report; if there be any virtue, and if there be any praise, think on these things," (KJV).

Though we have the mind of Christ, we still have a choice in what we choose to think about. At this moment in time, am I going to think about what I know to be true, or am I going to entertain a lie because of my feelings? Am I going to think about something honest or dishonest? Am I going to think about what is fair and just or am I going to think about that which is not fair (and perhaps even act in a way that is unjust)? My choice. Am I going to think about something pure or will I entertain that which I shouldn't look at, read, or listen to, much less think about? Will I think about that which is lovely or not? Will I choose to think about something that is good, of good report or that which is evil? Will I think about that which is virtuous or vile? Again, my choice. What about the last one, praise? Will I choose to think about that which is worthy of praise (including my Lord, Himself) or will I think about base, vulgar, or low things?

Romans 12:2 says, "And be not conformed to this world: but be ye transformed by the renewing of your mind, that ye may prove what is that good, and acceptable, and perfect, will of God," (KJV). If we wish to become mature and get beyond childish thinking, we need to choose to allow ourselves to be transformed, or changed, and actually renew our minds. That involves taking every thought captive and choosing instead to think good thoughts rather than allowing ourselves to be led (often astray!) by our emotions.

II Corinthians 10:3-6 says, "The world is unprincipled. It's dog-eat-dog out there! The world doesn't fight fair. But we don't live or fight our battles that way—never have and never will. The tools of our trade aren't for marketing or manipulation, but they are for demolishing that entire massively corrupt culture. We use our powerful God-tools for smashing warped philosophies, tearing down barriers erected against the truth of God, fitting every loose thought and emotion and impulse into the structure of life shaped by Christ. Our tools are ready at hand for clearing the ground of every obstruction and building lives of obedience into maturity," (MSG).

Take a few moments to digest the verses above. No one can argue against the world being unprincipled. Look at the crime rate. However, we don't live by the world's standards. Our standards are much, much higher. We aren't out to sell this great message of salvation. Jesus already paid all the cost necessary. When we choose to use our 'powerful God-tools' the people around us start to change, our world starts to change—for the better. We take the time to keep our thoughts, emotions, and impulses from running loose, for the glory of God and the blessing of others.

Think about times you have let your emotions, thoughts, or impulses run amok. Basically, when we allow our emotions, thoughts, or impulses to run rampant without check, we are allowing ourselves to be taken over by them, instead of submitting ourselves to Jesus. That is a dangerous place to be. If we truly want to become mature, we must fit our thoughts, emotions, and impulses into the 'structure of life shaped by Christ'. We've got the tools 'ready at hand'. Instead of allowing ourselves to be taken over by our base natures, let's clear some ground. Let's get rid of those obstructions that keep us from realizing the glorious miraculous life God has for us.

John Willison said, "He cures the mind of its blindness, the heart of its hardness, the nature of its perseverance (being argumentative), the will of its backwardness, the memory its slipperiness, the conscience of its benumbness (uncaring about consequences), and the affections of their disorder (craving things that are bad for us), all according to His gracious promises."

God wants you to not only defeat fear forever, but to replace it with something greater. Ezekiel 36:26-27 says, "A new heart also will I give you, and a new spirit will I put within you: and I will take away the stony heart out of your flesh, and I will give you an heart of flesh. And I will put my spirit within you, and cause you to walk in my statutes, and ye shall keep my judgments, and do them," (KJV).

As you grow in maturity, your priorities change. Just as you grew to adulthood, your priorities changed. When we have a new heart and a new spirit, we have the power to do things beyond our wildest dreams. That's what God has in store for us, joy unspeakable, peace unfathomable, and love unstoppable. Instead of anger, we speak peace. Instead of fear, we speak faith. Instead of hate, we speak love. In the face of the impossible, we have hope, unshakable hope.

Let me give an explicit example of changing priorities. I knew that God had called me to write this book. However, I was letting my responsibilities slip. My husband asked me about it one evening. He said, 'Which is more important to you this book or your children?' Now, in that moment, I had two choices. I could get angry and argue with him or I could humbly admit that I had indeed let some of my responsibilities slip. He wasn't questioning my calling. He was questioning my priorities. My first priority is to Jesus, giving Him time and sharing my life with Him. My second priority is to my husband, valuing him. My third is to my children, showing them that I love them. After that comes the book, work, ministry responsibilities, home management, etc. All of those things come in fourth place as far as priorities are concerned.

You see, all the accomplishments in the world, even if they are 'for God' mean absolutely nothing if my husband and children don't feel important. Of course, I could still write the book. My husband wasn't telling me to abandon it. He was telling me that our children need me, that he needed me. I prayed about fixing my priorities and ordering my life according to God's ideas and everything fell into place. My husband commented on it the very next day. God is a god of order, not chaos. By following His lead, and by leaning on Him for strength and direction, I can do whatever He calls me to do. I can be that miracle to myself—and so can you!

In this chapter, we discussed what it means to grow in maturity. We talked about the necessity of spending time every day reading the Bible and praying, so we can 'grow, grow, grow'. I quoted several Scriptures and discussed the importance of submitting ourselves to Christ and not allowing ourselves to sin, in fact, choosing to not sin. I shared some thoughts about how to change our thinking and the importance of allowing our priorities to fit with God's. I have no doubt that you can defeat fear forever. I did it. There's no reason why you can't do it too. God can and will make you a miracle. Just submit to Him and allow Him to change you.

Joy Haney in her excellent book, *At the Master's Feet*, said, "Saul, the persecutor, became Paul, the preacher. Peter, the fisherman, became the Apostle Peter. Mary Magdalene, the woman with seven devils, became the first witness of the resurrection. Anyone who has an encounter with Jesus Christ will never be the same. There will be some kind of change." All of these people became miracles not only to themselves but to the entire world. The same can happen to you. Just submit everything to Jesus and watch Him work—for you!

Chapter 9
Defeat Fear—Forever

To get the victory is one thing, to keep it is quite another. Several years ago, my husband and I moved into a house that had an in ground swimming pool. Sounds nice, yes? Unfortunately, this house was located in the mountains of Virginia. The season for swimming wasn't very long. The back yard was full of lots of tall trees. Also, the previous owners had already moved away to another state and weren't able to maintain the pool. It was a total mess. So, my husband and several neighbors spent many, many hours cleaning out the pool, hauling wheelbarrow after wheelbarrow of leaves out.

My point in telling this story is this, just as in cleaning out a pool, getting the victory over fear is a big deal. Once you've gotten that victory, you have something to be proud of. However, although that pool looked beautiful after that initial cleaning, we still had to maintain it. It is the same in KEEPING your victory over fear. The good news is maintenance isn't that hard if you keep doing it daily.

In the Bible, Acts 2, the apostles and the 120 people were all filled with the Holy Ghost on the day of Pentecost. Then, later on, it talks about some of the same people being 'filled'. Acts 4:31 says, "After this prayer, the meeting place shook, and they were all filled with the Holy Spirit. Then they preached the word of God with boldness," (NLT). This verse isn't just talking about people being filled with the Holy Ghost for the first time. This verse includes everybody. 'All' means 'all'. 'They were ALL filled with the Holy Spirit.' Acts 13:52 says, "And the disciples were continually filled [throughout their souls] with joy and the Holy Spirit," (AMP). The disciples were initially filled with the Holy Spirit back in Jerusalem in Acts 2:38. Here it says they were 'continually' filled [throughout their souls]. If the disciples (apostles) needed to be continually filled, so do we.

I want continuous power in my life, continuous joy, continuous peace, and continuous love. I want to be that miracle to myself and to the world. The thing is I cannot have continuous anything without the help of the Lord. Isaiah 40:13 says, "But they that wait upon the Lord shall renew their strength; they shall mount up with wings as eagles; they shall run, and not be weary; and they shall walk, and not faint," (KJV). The key in the verse above is WAITING on the Lord.

Psalm 112:7 says, "He shall not be afraid of evil tidings; his heart is firmly fixed, trusting (leaning on and being confident) in the Lord," (AMP).

When we keep our hearts on the Lord, when we wait upon Him, we get the power to do amazing things. We don't have to be afraid. When we are continually filled with the Spirit of the living God, there is no room for fear.

Pastor Robert Kaske preached recently about a large, delicious meal. He said that if a person is completely full after a meal he has no room for a dessert, even if it's a favorite. It doesn't even look tempting. That is what we need spiritually. We need to be so full of God's Spirit that the things of this world no longer tempt us or intimidate us. Having continuous power is simply being continuously filled with the Spirit of God.

Pastor Kaske said that certain conditions must be met in order to have continuous power in our lives. We must desire it, we must surrender our wills to Jesus, we must obey God, and we must confess when we sin.

"You're blessed when you've worked up a good appetite for God. He's food and drink in the best meal you'll ever eat," Matthew 5:6 (MSG). This is the desire I mentioned above. When you desire more of Jesus, you will be filled—to overflowing!

"So here's what I want you to do, God helping you: Take your everyday, ordinary life—your sleeping, eating, going-to-work, and walking-around life—and place it before God as an offering. Embracing what God does for you is the best thing you can do for him. Don't become so well-adjusted to your culture that you fit into it without even thinking. Instead, fix your attention on God. You'll be changed from the inside out. Readily recognize what he wants from you, and quickly respond to it. Unlike the culture around you, always dragging you down to its level of immaturity, God brings the best out of you, develops well-formed maturity in you," Romans 12:1-2 (MSG). This is surrender. When we willingly, consciously, continuously surrender ourselves to Him, He blesses us and fills us more and more.

"Here's how we can be sure that we know God in the right way: Keep his commandments," I John 2:2-3 (MSG). This is obedience. Keeping God's commandments are not limited to the 10 commandments. This verse means keeping God's teachings and precepts. Jesus had a lot to say about how we were to live our lives, loving God and others being the two most important. The bottom line is that we are not to just look in the Bible and mindlessly obey, we are to lovingly search God's Word and seek to do all that we can to please Him. Just as parents have certain rules for the benefit of their children, God has rules and commands to benefit and even bless us. He loves us. We can show our love for Him by seeking Him and working to obey Him every moment of our lives.

"If we claim that we're free of sin, we're only fooling ourselves. A claim like that is errant nonsense. On the other hand, if we admit our sins—make a clean breast of them—he won't let us down; he'll be true to himself. He'll forgive our sins and purge us of all wrongdoing," I John 1:8-9 (MSG). This is the confession. I'll say it again, if you mess up, fess up. The great thing is confessing our sins is the first step in getting free of them. When we admit we were wrong, we gain the power to change and not make the same mistake again and again and again.

One thing I struggle with is my own sense of self worth. Satan likes to get in and say that if I mess up, I am worthless and no longer worthy of love. The truth is God loves me so much that He died for me. My husband loves me. (He bought ME boots for Father's Day!) My children love me. Just because I FEEL so strongly that I'm not worthy of love doesn't make it true. Also, just because I don't feel loved doesn't make that true either. Feelings are meant to be our servants, not the other way around. We are to lead our feelings, capturing every thought, every feeling, and submitting it to Christ. When we do that, we don't fall into the pits Satan digs for us. Just because I don't feel Jesus' Spirit in me doesn't mean that He's not there. He gave me His Spirit and I have proof! Any time I want, I can start praying in tongues and praising Him. That is my proof, just as it was for the apostles 2000 years ago.

How can we have continuous power in our lives? Pastor Kaske answers this with three things, meeting conditions (desire, surrender, obedience, and confession), asking for power (Jesus wants to give us His power!), and simply trusting God for it. Isaiah 26:3 says, "You {Jesus} will guard him and keep him in perfect and constant peace whose mind [both its inclination and its character] is stayed on You, because he commits himself to You, leans on You, and hopes confidently in You," (AMP). Isaiah 40:31 says, "But they that wait upon the Lord shall renew their strength; they shall mount up with wings as eagles; they shall run, and not be weary; and they shall walk, and not faint," (KJV).

Recently, my husband preached a sermon entitled 'Power and Peace'. His whole point in his message was that God wants to do a work greater than you or I can handle. That's where the adventure begins! That's where YOU get to become a miracle! How was David able to say, "Yea, though I walk through the valley of the shadow of death, I will fear no evil..."? (Psalm 23) The answer is simple, "for Thou art with me." We can trust Him with the situations that are out of our control!

God has so many promises for us. I think one of the sweetest is the promise of 'sonship'. Galatians 3:26 says, "For ye are all the children of God by faith in Christ Jesus," (KJV). We are the sons and daughters of the Most High God, King of kings, Lord of lords. The fact is that through Jesus we become royalty, princes and princesses. Royalty behave a certain way, with a certain amount of dignity and confidence. There have been plenty of 'rags to riches' stories, but what does that mean? In Jesus, we have gone from filthy rags to eternal riches beyond all imagination. We are blessed both here and in the life to come.

A true prince or princess realizes that he or she is not to be served, but rather to serve his or her people. Jesus, the King of kings, is our perfect example of what true royalty looks like. He was never arrogant. He loved and served without complaining. He never forgot Who He was or what His true purpose was, yet He still took time to minister to people.

What on earth does the above have to do with defeating fear in my own life? Actually, it has everything to do with it. When I spend time loving, serving, and ministering to others, I don't have time to be afraid—of anything! It's not about forgetting self so much. It's about truly realizing who you are in Christ and learning to truly love others as you learn to love yourself. It's not about losing myself so much as it is finding myself in Christ. The focus is no longer on myself, but on Jesus and all the people around me that He has put in my life. It's realizing that that verse in Philippians 4:13 is absolutely true, "I CAN do all things through Christ Who strengthens me."

John 1:12 says, "But to all who believed him and accepted him, he gave the right to become children of God," (NLT). Have you believed? Have you accepted Him? Have you been born again of the water and the Spirit (John 3:5)? If you have had this beautiful experience like no other, then you can claim sonship. You can claim your royal right to be called a child of God Almighty.

Okay, so what does that have to do with defeating fear forever? Well, in order to reach a goal you have to know three things: where (or in this case what/who) you are, where you are going, and how to get there. You need to realize where you are at spiritually. You need to realize who and what you are spiritually. If your feelings don't match what the truth of the Bible says, then you need to boot those feelings out of your head in Jesus' name!

You need to know where you are going, what you are becoming. What is your goal for your life? What do you want to look like next year? In the next five years? In the next five minutes? You can't get to the moon if you don't aim for it. What does Jesus want for you? Do you believe you can have that? If not, pray God to help your unbelief! He will!

Now, I've spent the last nine chapters telling you how to defeat fear forever, but I hope that is only one of many goals you have for yourself. Jesus not only delivered you from your past, He also delivered you for your present and future. He has awesome plans for you. Don't sell yourself and Jesus short by not believing. Jesus could do nothing in His own hometown because of the people's unbelief. In other cities and towns He was able to do many, many miracles, because of the people's faith. As you trust God, He will grow your faith. You will start to become that amazing miracle to yourself. I know, because I am experiencing that too. I can't claim credit. I can only claim to trust Him. He has asked me to simply trust and obey Him and I have seen Him do the impossible. He comes through, every time, as long as I continue to trust. It's an amazing adventure, one I wouldn't trade for anything this world has to offer!

I Chronicles 29:11 says, "Thine, O Lord, is the greatness, and the power, and the glory, and the victory, and the majesty: for all that is in the heaven and in the earth is thine; thine is the kingdom, O Lord, and thou art exalted as head above all," (KJV). When we Christians start to realize just how great our God is, fear melts away, powerless. With God, the impossible things He asks us to do become possible—in partnership with Him. That's the key: We must walk WITH God. Our very lives must be in constant communication with him. It is then that we become untouchable!

Psalm 989:1 says, "O sing unto the Lord a new song; for He hath done marvelous things: His right hand, and His holy arm, hath gotten Him the victory," (KJV). God doesn't need us; He wants to be with us. He gave His precious blood so that we might be able to be with Him. Jesus can have the victory without any human at all, yet, instead, He chose to share His victory with us. In fact, we are both the victor and the prize. He enables us to be the miracle!

Isaiah 25:8 says, "He will swallow up death in victory; and the Lord God will wipe away tears from off all faces; and the rebuke of His people shall He take away from off all the earth: for the Lord hath spoken it," (KJV). Jesus already has the victory. He spoke it, just as He spoke the world into existence. It WILL come to pass. However, you and I have a choice as to whether or not we will share in the victory with Him.

When we choose to walk with the Lord, we submit our wills to His. We submit our thoughts and emotions to Him. My husband and I were discussing this not too long ago and we coined some new phrases for us: We can walk in 'victory mode' or in 'cater-to-your-emotions mode'. It's a struggle and a choice we all have to make many times every day of our lives.

Victory mode is unselfish. When I walk in victory mode I am fully submitted to the Lord. I am walking with Him and in His Holy Spirit. That doesn't mean I don't have my own thoughts. It's a partnership. However, I choose to follow His leading, rather than going off my own way.

The world says, 'Follow your heart.' 'Do what feels right.' The Bible says, "The foolishness of man perverteth his way: and his heart fretteth against the Lord," Proverbs 19:3 (KJV). "There are many devices in a man's heart; nevertheless the counsel of the Lord, that shall stand," Proverbs 19:21 (KJV).

We can't trust our feelings. They will lead us wrong. Again in Proverbs 14:12, it says, "There is a way that seemeth right unto a man, but the end thereof are the ways of death," (KJV). Think about it. Anytime I've acted selfishly, the good feelings I had did not last long. In fact, most of the time, I didn't have any good feelings. I just felt miserable.

Here is my hope: "For whatsoever is born of God overcometh the world: and this is the victory that overcometh the world, even our faith," I John 5:4 (KJV). I know I've been born of God. I've been born of the water and the Spirit like Jesus talked about to Nicodemus (John 3:5). I've been baptized in Jesus' name just like Peter preached on the day of Pentecost (Acts 2:38). I know this because I have evidence. I felt the water as I went under. I heard Jesus' name spoken by my pastor and there were many witnesses who saw it. I've been filled with (or baptized in or born of) the Spirit. I have evidence for this too. I've spoken in tongues as the Spirit gave utterance. I heard myself speak. I've spoken in tongues many times since then and others have heard it. Again this is found in Acts 2:38 and throughout the book of Acts. This, however, is only the beginning.

Remember when I talked about seeing yourself as a miracle? Because of this incredible journey I've embarked on with Jesus, I've been privileged to see many miracles. When we are born again, we aren't just born for ourselves; we're born to bring hope and miracles to other people around us.

One of the ministries my husband and I do is visiting sick people in the hospital. One day, I went to visit another lady in our church who was very sick and rather depressed. The flap in her throat no longer worked properly, so she couldn't eat. The food would end up in her lungs and she would die. So, she was on a feeding tube. When I walked into her hospital room, we talked for a little while, then, I asked if I could pray for her. As I put my hands gently on her head and shoulder, I felt the Lord asking me to tell her something. Unsure of myself at the time, I spoke in tongues, then waited for the interpretation. Over and over again, the Lord told me to tell her not to give up. I said it at least four times! (At the time, I wondered if this was the Lord of some strange pizza from the night before.) After I had finished praying, I needed to get back home, so I left. Several days later, she called me. I didn't know this, but when she was in the hospital, she was seriously considering suicide. She said the only thing that kept her from it was those words repeated over and over, 'Don't give up. Don't give up. Don't give up. Don't give up!'

There are three voices going on in our heads all the time, our own, the enemy, and the voice of the Lord. Jesus will never lead us wrong. He will never tell us to do something that goes against His Word, the Bible. The enemy delights in crippling us, hurting us, causing us to fall and hurt deep inside. Even our own emotions lead us down a road that isn't so good. Our emotions cause us to attack the very people who love and care for us the most. We believe the lies of Satan and think people are out to get us. The Bible says the truth will set us free. I want to walk WITH Jesus. I want to walk in 'Victory mode'. My thoughts and emotions need to walk with Jesus and submit to Him. I certainly don't want my thoughts and emotions to partner with Satan! However, that is exactly what happens when I allow myself to walk in 'cater-to-your-emotions mode'.

Recently, a friend of ours died. He left behind a beautiful wife and three small boys. My heart cries out why? Why didn't God heal him? The Lord answered me through my daughter. She said, 'At least now he is with Jesus.' Thinking of that really put things into perspective. Why do allow my emotions to guide me? Why have I ever gotten impatient with the kids? How much time will I get with them? How much time do I get with my incredible husband? I should bless and inspire and encourage and love them every moment of every day. I can only do that through walking WITH God, submitting to His Spirit, and staying in 'Victory mode'.

I Corinthians 15:54-55 says, "So when this corruptible shall have put on incorruption, and this mortal shall have put on immortality, then shall be brought o pass the saying that is written, Death is swallowed up in victory. O death, where is thy sting? O grave, where is thy victory?"

(KJV). This is the victory we live and die for. This life is far from easy, but we have a choice in how we choose to live it—'Victory mode' or 'cater-to-your-emotions mode'.

Galatians 5:16-25 says, "My counsel is this: Live freely, animated and motivated by God's Spirit. Then you won't feed the compulsions of selfishness. For there is a root of sinful self-interest in us that is at odds with a free spirit, just as the free spirit is incompatible with selfishness. These two ways of life are antithetical, so that you cannot live at times one way and at times another way according to how you feel on any given day. Why don't you choose to be led by the Spirit and so escape the erratic compulsions of a law-dominated existence?

"It is obvious what kind of life develops out of trying to get your own way all the time: repetitive, loveless, cheap sex; a stinking accumulation of mental and emotional garbage; frenzied and joyless grabs for happiness; trinket gods; magic-show religion; paranoid loneliness; cutthroat competition; all-consuming-yet-never-satisfied wants; a brutal temper; an impotence to love or be loved; divided homes and divided lives; small-minded and lopsided pursuits; the vicious habit of depersonalizing everyone into a rival; uncontrolled and uncontrollable addictions; ugly parodies of community. I could go on.

"This isn't the first time I have warned you, you know. If you use your freedom this way, you will not inherit God's kingdom.

"But what happens when we live God's way? He brings gifts into our lives, much the same way that fruit appears in an orchard—things like affection for others, exuberance about life, serenity. We develop a willingness to stick with things, a sense of compassion in the heart, and a conviction that a basic holiness permeates things and people. We find ourselves involved in loyal commitments, not needing to force our way in life, able to marshal and direct our energies wisely.

"Legalism is helpless in bringing this about; it only gets in the way. Among those who belong to Christ, everything connected with getting our own way and mindlessly responding to what everyone else calls necessities is killed off for good—crucified.

"Since this is the kind of life we have chosen, the life of the Spirit, let us make sure that we do not just hold it as an idea in our heads or a sentiment in our hearts, but work out its implications in every detail of our lives," (MSG).

This is how to defeat fear and keep on defeating it. This is how to live in victory. This is how to fight. This is also a choice. Will you choose to walk in 'Victory mode' or 'cater-to-your-emotions mode'? The fight is not with each other. It is with our own flesh and Satan, himself. I want to win, but winning takes work. It takes some good, old-fashioned fight. The easy way is to let my emotions control me. It's easy to go with the 'flow' of the world. Why would Satan fight us if we're already doing what he wants? He enjoys tormenting us, but he will not fight us if we are following our own desires and selfish wants. In fact, he'll cheer us on! He'll cheer us right into eternal darkness, fear, death, and the ultimate agony of defeat.

I choose to fight. I choose to walk WITH God. I choose to submit my thoughts and emotions today, right now, this moment, to Jesus. I choose to walk in Victory mode! I choose to defeat fear right now and forever more!

What will you choose?

Conclusion

"Come to me, all you who are weary and burdened, and I will give you rest. Take my yoke upon you and learn from me, for I am gentle and humble in heart, and you will find rest for your souls. For my yoke is easy and my burden is light," Matthew 11:28-30 (NIV).

Fighting and defeating anything, especially fear, can be tough. I've heard it said, 'Work smarter, not harder' and it's true, even in this. I used to think that walking in the Spirit consistently was hard work, but it's not. Jesus said that His yoke is easy. Walking in His Spirit is easy, not hard. The work He gives us can be challenging, but it's not 'hard'. His burdens are light.

Trying to go it alone, carrying all your burdens all by yourself is hard. Trying to walk in a different direction than the one Jesus is walking in is hard. Carrying burdens you were never meant to carry is hard. Walking WITH Jesus (and submitting your will to Him), however, is easy.

My daughter has had this love/hate relationship with math, especially Algebra. Part of the problem is she likes to just blaze through everything, rather than being slow and careful. For a novel, such as Pride and Prejudice by Jane Austen, blazing through is okay if the comprehension is there. For my daughter, she excels in literature. However, math requires slowing down. The other part of her problem is attitude. When something isn't immediately easy, she gets frustrated and thinks she can't do it. This compounds the problem and makes it all worse.

Finally, my husband suggested a rather radical solution. I would read whatever chapter she was on in her textbook first, and then she would work on it and ask any questions she had. At first, I admit that I wasn't very enthusiastic about the idea. I've got enough on my plate without more 'homework'. On the other hand, my daughter's education is extremely important and we needed to help her. So, I started reading the chapters ahead of her.

It's rather nuts what happened. I've been reading the chapters and was able to figure out all the problems without any difficulty and my daughter hasn't really needed my help much at all! What had happened is that she felt alone. Her father and I knew that she could do the work without our help, but she didn't believe that. Once she knew that someone else had gone through the chapter and had it all figured out before she was expected to, all the pressure that she had felt was gone. She wasn't alone anymore. I could help her if she got truly stuck.

My husband does essentially the same thing with his violin students. The parents learn to play the violin along with their children. For the first month, the children don't get lessons, only the parents. The parents see firsthand just how difficult learning to play the violin is. The children, through observation, learn more in that month than they would have had my husband taught them first! (The children also get great enjoyment out of correcting Mom's or Dad's posture, finger position, bow hold, etc.)

The interesting things that result from this are that parents are challenged and gain an understanding of what their children are attempting. Parents learn to be much more encouraging as well.

As applied to Algebra, another result of doing this course with my daughter is that her confidence (and mine) has soured upwards. She knows for herself that she can do it. It's even rather 'easy' for her. I am a bit surprised at how well I'm remembering it all. I never hated math, but now, it's actually fun. I'm enjoying my homework. The Lord has used this to help me bond in a new way with my daughter.

What on earth has this to do with defeating fear? Or walking in the Spirit? Well, actually, quite a lot. Remember when I said to work smarter, not harder? Reading a couple of chapters of Algebra a week is certainly a lot easier than being hit with a difficult problem and trying to remember math from 15 years ago in ten minutes or less. When I tried to help her, I felt stressed—and so did she. Now, it's easy. Work smarter, not harder. Sure, it takes some time for me to read the chapters, but this is so very much easier! This yoke is easy compared to what we were doing before, and this burden is so much lighter.

Truly, in order to defeat fear forever, it all comes down to one simple thing—TRUST. Who and what are you going to trust? Are you going to trust Jesus or your feelings and emotions? Are you going to trust what the Bible says or what you happen to be feeling (and what Satan is whispering into your ear) at the moment? Now, most people would say, rather huffily, "Of course I'm going to trust Jesus and the Bible!" Unfortunately, that's awfully easy to say and much harder to actually live out in your life. Who will you trust more, Jesus or yourself?

There's a story about a little girl who had a lovely fake pearl watch that she treasured greatly. Every night her daddy tucked her into bed and asked her if she would give him the watch. She always replied, "Oh Daddy, you know I love you, but I can't give up my watch." He smiled a little sadly and gently kissed her forehead before leaving the room.

One night, when her daddy came into the room, the little girl was sitting up in her bed crying. Wordlessly, she handed the fake pearl watch to her father. He just smiled, kissed her gently and tucked her into her bed, taking the watch with him.

The next morning, sitting beside her alarm clock, was a real pearl watch waiting for the little girl. When she saw the watch, she couldn't help the little squeal of delight. Her daddy came in and said, "I couldn't give you the real thing until you were willing to give up the fake one."

The little girl in this story had a hard time trusting her daddy. She thought she knew best. She wanted to hold onto what she knew rather than letting go and trusting. How often does God ask us to walk with Him in faith and just see what He has in store for us? Sometimes it's really hard to let go of those things we treasure, even if they aren't worth treasuring. Yet, when we choose to trust, we are always blessed. It may not be in the way we expect, but we are blessed never the less.

Another story deals with pride. A friend of ours is a fairly new Christian and compares her life to driving a car with the Lord. After she decided to trust the Lord, she thought of Him as being the one in the driver's seat with her just sitting next to Him enjoying the ride. However, one day, she decided that she had this whole 'Christian' thing figured out and she could drive for awhile. So, (figuratively), she shoved the Lord out of the way, and took over. He patiently sat off to the side and let her drive. He tried to warn her that it wasn't a good idea, but she wouldn't listen. "I've got this, Lord," she said. Unfortunately, she didn't see the sharp turn or the tree up ahead. She plowed right into it. The Lord helped her and forgave her and she learned that the Lord was a much better driver of her life. Every time she tried to take over, it usually ended in disaster. Now, she is content to just let the Lord drive.

The lesson in that story is again, who will you trust with your life, yourself or the Lord? It's so easy to let pride creep in and decide you don't need the Lord's help, but that's usually right before disaster strikes. When we choose to submit our lives and our wills to the Lord, things run much more smoothly. We are free to become the miracles we were created to be and free to bless others. Submitting to the Lord is not always fun, but it is always right.

Recently, Pastor Kaske preached a sermon called Fearless Living, based on Joshua 1:1-18. This takes place right after Moses had died and Joshua was set to take over the leadership of the people of Israel. They were about to (finally) enter the promise land and take possession of it. Joshua was a little nervous. So, the Lord spoke to him and helped him.

Joshua 1:1-2 says, "After the death of Moses the LORD's servant, the LORD spoke to Joshua son of Nun, Moses' assistant. He said, [2] "Moses my servant is dead. Therefore, the time has come for you to lead these people, the Israelites, across the Jordan River into the land I am giving them," (NLT).

Pastor Kaske's first principle of fearless living was to 'Let Go of the Past'. When the Lord spoke to Joshua, the first thing He said was, "Moses my servant is dead." Joshua needed to release himself from the past and all of his and his people's past mistakes. If we can't let go of the past, we can't move forward.
We all have things in our past that we're ashamed of. However, in recalling those things, are you being convicted or condemned? If you've already repented and done what you could to make it right, it's all 'under the blood of Jesus' and needs to stay there!

Joshua 1:3-9 says, "I promise you what I promised Moses: 'Wherever you set foot, you will be on land I have given you—[4] from the Negev wilderness in the south to the Lebanon mountains in the north, from the Euphrates River in the east to the Mediterranean Sea in the west, including all the land of the Hittites.' [5] No one will be able to stand against you as long as you live. For I will be with you as I was with Moses. I will not fail you or abandon you.

[6] "Be strong and courageous, for you are the one who will lead these people to possess all the land I swore to their ancestors I would give them. [7] Be strong and very courageous. Be careful to obey all the instructions Moses gave you. Do not deviate from them, turning either to the right or to the left. Then you will be successful in everything you do. [8] Study this Book of Instruction continually. Meditate on it day and night so you will be sure to obey everything written in it. Only then will you prosper and succeed in all you do. [9] This is my command—be strong and courageous! Do not be afraid or discouraged. For the LORD your God is with you wherever you go."

Pastor Kaske's second principle is to 'Trust God's Promises in the Present'. God made several promises to Joshua, but those would be meaningless if Joshua just did nothing. He had to get up and MOVE. He had to trust that God was going to give them the land, that God was going to be with them, with him. 'For the Lord your God is with you wherever you go.' The key to fearless living is FAITH (or trust). Psalm 56:11 says, I will trust you, i.e. I CHOOSE to trust You, Lord. That means, even when it looks scary, I will trust that the Lord knows what He's doing and where we're going. I will submit my will to His and trust and obey. I will move according to His leading—and it will be awesome!

Pastor Kaske's third principle is 'Study God's Word for Guidance in the Future'. If we have our minds fixed on the Lord, our problems don't seem nearly so large. "Draw near to God and He will draw near to you…" James 4:8. The preceding verse is interesting as well. "Submit yourselves therefore to God. Resist the devil and he will flee from you," James 4:7 (KJV). It's great to say to Satan, 'Get out of here!' But, if we don't submit to God, our command is meaningless. We don't have any power in and of ourselves over Satan. In a way, the Lord Himself is our armor. Without Him, it's a little like going into battle unarmed, without any weapons at all. Of course, we'll get creamed. The good news is that the Lord wants to be with us. He wants us to 'be strong and courageous'. He wants great things for us. However, just as a drill driver doesn't work very well without the battery pack, we don't work very well unless we're plugged in to our Power Source, the Lord Himself.

How can we be 'plugged in'? Well, we can start with prayer and studying God's Word, the Bible. I love Psalm 1:2-3, "Instead you thrill to GOD's Word, you chew on Scripture day and night. You're a tree replanted in Eden, bearing fresh fruit every month, never dropping a leaf, always in blossom," (MSG). Basically, what this means is that if we will study God's Word and apply it to our lives, actually living it out, not just merely reading it, we will have success. I don't know about you, but I like that!

Here is a nice way to get more out of studying God's Word: SPECS, five questions based on Psalm 119:105.

Sin to confess and forsake?
Promises to claim?
Examples to follow?
Command to obey?
Stumbling block to avoid?

Every time you read a passage of Scripture, ask yourself these five questions. It's so exciting to learn more and more about the Lord and what He wants to do in our lives and the lives of those around us. As we apply the truths we learn, our lives change.

When we pray and study God's Word, the Bible, and apply it to our lives, our trust in God (faith) grows. As our trust grows, we find we have less and less room for fear. It's like darkness versus light. No matter how much darkness you try to capture by going outside at night, when you step inside, the darkness is scattered by the light. As we work to fill our lives with more and more light, learning to be ever more and more 'full of the Spirit', the darkness is literally displaced, pushed out.

The past several weeks have been a rather difficult for me. My husband had a partially collapsed lung, all five of my children were sick with fevers and two of them had pneumonia. It was all rather awful. Yet, I know the Lord was with me. I could feel His constant presence. I had a choice. Was I going to allow myself to trust my circumstances and let go of the Lord's peace? Or, was I going to trust the Lord and allow Him to comfort, encourage, and direct me? Well, let's just say some days were better than others. You see, it wasn't just a onetime decision. It was a daily choice, sometimes a moment by moment choice.

To top it all off, I nearly missed an important meeting for one of my part time jobs. (I had to teleconference in.) I had written the time down wrong on my calendar. I felt just awful about the whole thing. In fact, I spent the rest of the day kicking myself, until my husband pointed out that I just might be listening to my own pride. Ouch! He was right. Yes, I really did blow it, but the world didn't end. This is one of those instances where I have to say simply, I'm sorry, and move on. The Lord forgave me. I needed to forgive myself and let it go. (Let go of the past...) Hmm.

If I don't feel the Lord's peace, there's something wrong. He didn't go anywhere. I did. Now, how do I get back? Well, trust God's promises in the present... He said He would forgive me if I messed up and He'd help me to be better. Praise the Lord for that! I choose to trust the Lord even in my failures. He won't leave me. He loves me. He won't reject me when I choose to trust Him.

Remember the Intro and Chapter 1? I need to believe that 'I CAN do all things through Christ who strengthens me.' It's not some pseudo-Christian I-don't-believe-in-myself-but-I-believe-in-Jesus idea. It's about really trusting what He actually said in His Word, the Bible, and choosing to believe that over what I feel!

Is there anything else I need to do? Yes, study God's Word for guidance in the future... Again, when I choose to submit to God, He is faithful to me. He draws near to me and Satan runs. The darkness is pushed out by the Light. It's through prayer and studying God's Word that I am comforted and led. In this case, I just simply needed to let go of my failure and do my job to the best of my ability.

Fearless living isn't really hard. It's simply choosing to trust the Lord no matter what the circumstances around you are. Defeating fear is a battle, but it can be won. Submit your will to the Lord and He will bless you. Draw near to the

Light and the darkness has to flee. The more your life is filled with the light of Jesus, the less room there is for darkness. Just as the darkness shrinks away in a lighted room, so Fear shrinks away into nothingness.

Hebrews 11:1-2 says, "NOW FAITH is the assurance (the confirmation, the title deed) of the things [we] hope for, being the proof of things [we] do not see and the conviction of their reality [faith perceiving as real fact what is not revealed to the senses]. [2]For by [faith--trust and holy fervor born of faith] the men of old had divine testimony borne to them and obtained a good report," (AMP).

This is what faith is: assurance, confirmation, the title deed. Faith is proof in our hearts and conviction in our souls of what we can't necessarily see. Holy fervor is that faith put into action. These men (of old) weren't guided by their fears; they were guided by faith to do great and mighty things. They became miracles to themselves and others.

The Message Bible puts Hebrews 11:1- 2 this way, "The fundamental fact of existence is that this trust in God, this faith, is the firm foundation under everything that makes life worth living. It's our handle on what we can't see. The act of faith is what distinguished our ancestors, set them above the crowd."

144

I want to live a life that is set above the crowd. I want to live a life of peace, joy, and love. Gal 5:22-23 says, "But the Holy Spirit produces this kind of fruit in our lives: love, joy, peace, patience, kindness, goodness, faithfulness, gentleness, and self-control. There is no law against these things!" (NLT). The only way to produce this kind of fruit in my life is through submitting myself to the Lord and living my life His way. Psalm 1:1-2 says that I am blessed if I don't walk with sinners, but instead choose to walk with the Lord. In fact, it says in verse three that I will be successful in all that I do.

It all boils down to this: Success depends on me depending on the Lord! If I want to defeat fear forever, I have to simply depend on Jesus. It is then that light overcomes the darkness and I can enjoy my victory.

So, what will you do? Will you submit and depend on the Lord? It's your choice, no one else's. Choose right here, right now which way you will go. If you chose the Lord's way, keep on choosing the Lord's way. You will soon see yourself becoming much more than you could have ever imagined...

Christina Li is married to Charles Li, owner/operator of 'Charles Li Violins.' Together, they live in Rochester, Minnesota with their five children. Besides writing, Christina enjoys reading, machine knitting, and playing games with her family. She home-schools all five of her children, writes regularly for Perspectives Magazine, and serves as an Institutional Review Board member at Mayo Clinic. Her ministry duties include co-directing the choir, working with the Wednesday night Kid's Club, ministering to prisoners, teaching various Bible studies, ministering in various local nursing homes, and singing and playing the piano.

www.ingramcontent.com/pod-product-compliance
Lightning Source LLC
Chambersburg PA
CBHW072133280526
45788CB00002B/616